To Ma / Ruth

Some more Australian countryside.

Lots of Love + Happy Birthday

Phil / Son

July 1990

A Treasury of FAVOURITE AUSTRALIAN POEMS

A Treasury of
FAVOURITE AUSTRALIAN POEMS

VIKING O'NEIL

Viking O'Neil
Penguin Books Australia Ltd
487 Maroondah Highway, PO Box 257
Ringwood, Victoria 3134, Australia
Penguin Books Ltd
Harmondsworth, Middlesex, England
Viking Penguin Inc.
40 West 23rd Street, New York, N.Y. 10010, U.S.A.
Penguin Books Canada Limited
2801 John Street, Markham, Ontario, Canada L3R 1B4
Penguin Books (N.Z.) Ltd
182-190 Wairau Road, Auckland 10, New Zealand

First published by Currey O'Neil Ross Pty Ltd 1982
Reprinted 1983, 1984, 1986
This edition published by Penguin Books Australia Ltd 1987

10 9 8 7 6 5 4 3

Produced by Viking O'Neil
56 Claremont Street, South Yarra, Victoria 3141, Australia
A division of Penguin Books Australia Ltd

Designed and set in Australia
Printed in China through Bookbuilders Ltd

National Library of Australia
Cataloguing-in-Publication data

A Treasury of favourite Australian poems

ISBN 0 670 90031 1.

1. Australian poetry.

A821'008

CONTENTS

INTRODUCTION

Australia was a forbidding and alien place to the early colonists and convicts. Its sombre-leaved trees, dark blue skies and harsh, searingly hot interior were not regarded with much affection until one or two generations of Australian-born children had grown up in the bush.

The poetry of the nineteenth and even the early twentieth centuries helped to provide a vital bridge between this unfamiliar continent and its new inhabitants. It articulated Australians' growing feelings of their own national image, and helped them to come to terms with their strange land.

The themes of the heat, vastness, harshness and isolation of the Australian outback appear again and again in Australian poems such as Barcroft Boake's "Where the Dead Men Lie",

> Out in the wastes of the Never Never —
> That's where the dead men lie!
> There where the heat-waves dance forever —
> That's where the dead men lie!

and Will Ogilvie's "Drought",

> My road is fenced with bleached, white bones,
> and strewn with the blind, white sand,
> Beside me a suffering, dumb world moans
> On the breast of a lonely land.

But these themes are not always treated negatively. They are often softened by the poet's love of the Australian landscape and its people. The courageous characters of the outback — stockmen, drovers, shearers, bullockies, swaggies and selectors and their families — are the subjects of dozens of well-known Australian poems, such as Adam Lindsay Gordon's "The Sick Stockrider",

Hold hard, Ned! Lift me down once more, and lay me in the shade.
Old man, you've had your work cut out to guide
Both horses, and to hold me in the saddle when I sway'd
All through the hot, slow, sleepy, silent ride.

and Henry Lawson's "The Teams",

> With face half-hid by a broad-brimmed hat,
> That shades from the heat's white waves,
> And shouldered whip, with its green-hide plait,
> The driver plods with a gait like that
> Of his weary, patient slaves . . .
>
> He'll sometimes pause as a thing of form
> In front of a settler's door,
> And ask for a drink, and remark "It's warm".
> Or say "There's signs of a thunderstorm";
> But he seldom utters more.

Another recurring theme in Australian poetry is defiance towards the boss and a distrust of city toffs and politicians. Lawson, in particular, often returns to these ideas in poems such as "Andy's Gone with Cattle",

> Oh, who shall cheek the squatter now
> When he comes round us snarling?
> His tongue is growing hotter now
> Since Andy crossed the Darling.

and "The Men Who Made Australia",

There'll be royal times in Sydney for the Cuff and Collar Push . . .
But the men who made the land will not be there.

Charles Harpur was one of the first poets to describe the Australian landscape with accuracy and feeling. His "A

Mid-Summer Noon in the Australian Forest" perfectly captures the magical peace and drowsiness of a summer noon in the bush. Henry Kendall was another mid-nineteenth century poet to portray the bush with affection. His best-known poem "Bell-Birds" is still a fresh evocation of the sights and sounds of Australia's enchanting mountain creeks and glades.

The poems of Harpur and Kendall reflected a growing appreciation of the bush, but it was probably the famous poem, "My Country" by Dorothea Mackellar, which best succeeded in vocalising Australians' acceptance and pride in their land. This poem struck a chord in the hearts of Australians, and primary school children all over Australia had to learn it by heart in the 'forties and 'fifties.

Australia's earliest versifiers were the expatriate balladists who first described the plight of the convicts, and later the daring exploits of bushrangers and the hard but proud life of the man of the outback. The names of these poets are long forgotten but their poignant verses live on, as do popular work songs which began to emerge, such as "Click Go The Shears, Boys"

Against the background of a harsh, new pioneering nation with little time for frills or niceties, it is not surprising that some of Australia's best-known and most popular poems are not particularly profound or literary in style. But they are full of life and vigour and are the direct descendants of the lively ballads of the early eighteenth century.

Three such poems, which are held in great affection by most older Australians, are "The Man from Snowy River", "Clancy of the Overflow" and Australia's unofficial national anthem "Waltzing Matlida". All three are the works of prolific poet A.B. ("Banjo") Paterson. Significantly, the central figure in all these poems is a loner with his own brand of courage or bravado.

Paterson, together with C.J. Dennis (best known for his humourous masterpiece "The Sentimental Bloke") wrote much of Australia's best-loved and somehow, most essentially Australian poetry. Like many other Australian poets, most of their poems are written with the particular cadence and subtleties of Australian speech and many of them are suffused with what is regarded as typically Australian humour — dry and understated. The splendid poems of Henry Lawson are also in rough-hewn language and often tinged with humour. There can surely be few countries in the world to have such a high proportion of humourous poems among its "classics". Where else would the leading bards of the day ponder over such subjects as mothers-in-law (Dennis), bicycle-riding (Paterson) and the impossibility of trying to be a hero . . ."When Your Pants Begin to Go" (Lawson)?

Outstanding Australian poets such as Mary Gilmore, John Shaw Neilson, Judith Wright, Kenneth Slessor, A.D. Hope and many more have emerged this century, and the works of some of them are included here.

However this collection is by no means representative of modern Australian poetry. The poems have been chosen on the basis of their freshness, their special quality of "Australian-ness" and for their general popularity. Many first-class poems have been omitted because they did not fulfil these criteria. Understandably, the majority of poems to have gained widespread appeal among the people of Australia, were written some time ago. Modern poems have not yet had the chance to be widely read, nor to pass the test of time. The modern poems selected have been chosen because they add, in some way or another, to the overall picture of Australia and her people. Many of these poems are already being read and enjoyed by a new generation of Australian school children who may well grow up to regard them as well-loved "classics".

A MID-SUMMER NOON IN THE AUSTRALIAN FOREST

Charles Harpur

Not a sound disturbs the air,
There is quiet everywhere;
Over plains and over woods
What a mighty stillness broods!

All the birds and insects keep
Where the coolest shadows sleep;
Even the busy ants are found
Resting in their pebbled mound;
Even the locust clingeth now
Silent to the barky bough:
Over hills and over plains
Quiet, vast and slumbrous, reigns.

Only there's a drowsy humming
From yon warm lagoon slow coming:
'Tis the dragon-hornet — see!
All bedaubed resplendently,
Yellow on a tawny ground —
Each rich spot nor square nor round,
Rudely heart-shaped, as it were
The blurred and hasty impress there
Of a vermeil-crusted seal
Dusted o'er with golden meal.
Only there's a droning where
Yon bright beetle shines in air,
Tracks it in its gleaming flight
With a slanting beam of light,

[Rising in the . . .

Rising in the sunshine higher,
Till its shards flame out like fire.

Every other thing is still,
Save the ever-wakeful rill,
Whose cool murmur only throws
Cooler comfort round repose;
Or some ripple in the sea
Of leafy boughs, where, lazily,
Tired summer, in her bower
Turning with the noontide hour,
Heaves a slumbrous breath ere she
Once more slumbers peacefully.

O 'tis easeful here to lie
Hidden from noon's scorching eye,
In this grassy cool recess
Musing thus of quietness.

SOUTH OF MY DAYS

Judith Wright

South of my days' circle, part of my blood's country,
rises that tableland, high delicate outline
of bony slopes wincing under the winter,
low trees blue-leaved and olive, outcropping granite —
clean, lean, hungry country. The creek's leaf-silenced,
willow-choked, the slope a tangle of medlar and crab-apple
branching over and under, blotched with a green lichen;
and the old cottage lurches in for shelter.

O cold the black-frost night. The walls draw in to the warmth
and the old roof cracks its joints; the slung kettle
hisses a leak on the fire. Hardly to be believed that summer
will turn up again some day in a wave of rambler roses,
thrust its hot face in here to tell another yarn —
a story old Dan can spin into a blanket against the winter.
Seventy years of stories he clutches round his bones.
Seventy summers are hived in him like old honey.

Droving that year, Charleville to the Hunter,
nineteen-one it was, and the drought beginning;
sixty head left at the McIntyre, the mud round them
hardened like iron; and the yellow boy died
in the sulky ahead with the gear, but the horse went on,
stopped at the Sandy Camp and waited in the evening.
It was the flies we seen first, swarming like bees.
Came to the Hunter, three hundred head of a thousand —
cruel to keep them alive — and the river was dust.

Or mustering up in the Bogongs in the autumn
when the blizzards came early. Brought them down; we brought them
down, what aren't there yet. Or driving for Cobb's on the run
up from Tamworth — Thunderbolt at the top of Hungry Hill,
and I give him a wink. I wouldn't wait long, Fred,
not if I was you; the troopers are just behind,
coming for that job at the Hillgrove. He went like a luny,
him on his big black horse.

            Oh, they slide and they vanish
as he shuffles the years like a pack of conjurors' cards.
True or not, it's all the same; and the frost on the roof
cracks like a whip, and the back-log breaks into ash.
Wake, old man. This is winter, and the yarns are over.
No one is listening.
            South of my days' circle
I know it dark against the stars, the high lean country
full of old stories that still go walking in my sleep.

OUT BACK

Henry Lawson

The old year went, and the new returned, in the withering weeks of drought;
The cheque was spent that the shearer earned, and the sheds were all cut out;
The publican's words were short and few, and the publican's looks were black —
And the time had come, as the shearer knew, to carry his swag Out Back.

For time means tucker, and tramp you must, where the scrubs and plains are wide,
With seldom a track that a man can trust, or a mountain peak to guide;
All day long in the dust and heat — when summer is on the track —
With stinted stomachs and blistered feet, they carry their swags Out Back.

He tramped away from the shanty there, when the days were long and hot,
With never a soul to know or care if he died on the track or not.
The poor of the city have friends in woe, no matter how much they lack,
But only God and the swagmen know how a poor man fares Out Back.

He begged his way on the parched Paroo and the Warrego tracks once more,
And lived like a dog, as the swagmen do, till the western stations shore;
But men were many, and the sheds were full, for work in the town was slack —
The traveller never got hands in wool, though he tramped for a year Out Back.

In stifling noons when his back was wrung by its load, and the air seemed dead,
And the water warmed in the bag that hung to his aching arm like lead.
Or in times of flood, when plains were seas and the scrubs were cold and black,
He ploughed in mud to his trembling knees, and paid for his sins Out Back.

And dirty and careless and old he wore, as his lamp of hope grew dim;
He tramped for years, till the swag he bore seemed part of himself to him.
As a bullock drags in the sandy ruts, he followed the dreary track,
With never a thought but to reach the huts when the sun went down Out Back.

[It chanced one day . . .

It chanced one day when the north wind blew in his face like a furnace-breath,
He left the track for a tank he knew — 'twas a shorter cut to death;
For the bed of the tank was hard and dry, and crossed with many a crack,
And, oh! it's a terrible thing to die of thirst in the scrub Out Back.

A drover came, but the fringe of law was eastward many a mile;
He never reported the thing he saw, for it was not worth his while.
The tanks are full, and the grass is high in the mulga off the track,
Where the bleaching bones of a white man lie by his mouldering swag Out Back.

For time means tucker, and tramp they must, where the plains and scrubs are wide,
With seldom a track that a man can trust, or a mountain peak to guide;
All day long in the flies and heat the men of the outside track,
With stinted stomachs and blistered feet, must carry their swags Out Back.

OLD BOTANY BAY

Mary Gilmore

"I'm old
Botany Bay;
Stiff in the joints,
Little to say.

I am he
Who paved the way,
That you might walk
At your ease to-day;

I was the conscript
Sent to hell
To make in the desert
The living well;

I bore the heat,
I blazed the track —
Furrowed and bloody
Upon my back.

I split the rock;
I felled the tree:
The nation was —
Because of me!"

Old Botany Bay
Taking the sun
From day to day . . .
Shame on the mouth
That would deny
The knotted hands
That set us high!

MY COUNTRY

Dorothea Mackellar

The love of field and coppice,
Of green and shaded lanes,
Of ordered woods and gardens
Is running in your veins.
Strong love of grey-blue distance,
Brown streams and soft, dim skies —
I know, but cannot share it,
My love is otherwise.

I love a sunburnt country,
A land of sweeping plains,
Of ragged mountain ranges,
Of droughts and flooding rains.
I love her far horizons,
I love her jewel-sea,
Her beauty and her terror —
The wide brown land for me!

The stark white ring-barked forests,
All tragic to the moon,
The sapphire-misted mountains,
The hot gold hush of noon,
Green tangle of the brushes
Where lithe lianas coil,
And orchids deck the tree-tops,
And ferns the warm dark soil.

[Core of my heart . . .

Core of my heart, my country!
Her pitiless blue sky,
When, sick at heart, around us
We see the cattle die —
But then the grey clouds gather,
And we can bless again
The drumming of an army,
The steady soaking rain.

Core of my heart, my country!
Land of the rainbow gold,
For flood and fire and famine
She pays us back threefold.
Over the thirsty paddocks,
Watch, after many days,
The filmy veil of greenness
That thickens as we gaze . . .

An opal-hearted country,
A wilful, lavish land —
All you who have not loved her,
You will not understand —
Though Earth holds many splendours,
Wherever I may die,
I know to what brown country
My homing thoughts will fly.

THE WASTE LAND

F. J. H. Letters

There is no beauty in that land,
That rigid, staring scene,
Where distant ranges are not blue,
Nor closer mountains, green;
But bare and yellow, far and wide
Heave tidal waves of stone;
Where rippling wheat pursues no breeze
And flocks were never known,
No clouds convoy their mirrored selves
Across a brooding mere,
No midday skies alive with stars
In flinching streams appear;
No trees are white with fragrant foam,
Or beaten black with rain,
No garden feeds its flames with dew,
No orchards wax and wane;
And though at least the watered palm
Would shimmer fitly there,
Oasis and mirage alike
Have never plumed the air.

There is no music in that land,
Of birds, of beast, or faun;
No crickets chirr the evening in,
No larks flute up the dawn.
No volleying lion shakes a hill,
No reed sings with the breeze,
No muzzling bees stir bells of flowers

[To booming . . .

To booming harmonies.
No sea there alternates the tones
Of organ and of lute,
Or cataract blows its steady horn —
Was ever world as mute?
A desert that has never once
Heard swaying camel bells
Chant over its untraversed death
Their necromantic spells.

No passion gives that land a soul,
A vital, burning grace;
No memories soften to a dream
The rigour of its face.
No heroes' blood has signed those fields
With glory's crimson name,
Adventure never scrawled the hills
With honour or with shame,
Nor lover kissed a flushing maid
To pallor like his own,
In that inhuman, frigid land,
That wilderness of stone.
And yet — what loveliness of earth
In dawn, or dusk, or noon,
May match that palsied, glamorous waste,
The mountains of the moon!

WEST OF ALICE

W. E. ("Bill") Harney

We are travelling west of Alice Springs, and Sam is at the wheel;
Riding the diesel-grader I am watching its blade of steel
Roll back the dark-red sandy loam or grind the limestones grey,
And the wheels whirl in a red-dust swirl along the new highway.

We pass where Sturt-peas clothe the earth with a scarlet sweep of flowers,
And burst through green acacia-trees that send down golden showers;
The parakeelia's purple blooms are crushed in the dry, red sand
When the bright blade sweeps as the grader creeps over the stern, strange land.

The mulga, mallee, desert-oaks fall prostrate as we pass,
The lizards, pigeons, porcupines crouch low in stone and grass;
We brush the spinifex aside; tear down the bush-rat's shade,
And the desert mole in its sandhill hole digs faster from our blade.

The honey-ants are rooted out to roll upon the sand,
But ever the ramping, stamping fiend goes roaring through the land;
The tyres grind and the steel blade cuts the pads where camels trod
And claws at the ground of a stony mound where tribesmen praised their God.

We cross the desert rivers, formed when the world was new,
And churn to dust the fossil-bones of the giant kangaroo;
I wave to naked native kids upon Erldunda's plain,
And we fill our tank where the black men drank from rock-holes filled by rain.

We camp in Kulgera's weathered hills, scarred core of an ancient range,
Where the camp-fire flame throws out its light on a scene that is ever strange
As a dingo wails by the painted wall of a sacred cave near by
And the stars shine bright as we lie at night beneath a frosty sky.

We rise as mulga-parakeets go whirling through the dawn,
We see old star-man Manbuk rise from depths of midnight drawn;
We hear the grader's engine roar with Sam behind the wheel,
And I sing my song as we plunge along to the chatter of wheel and steel.

WHERE THE DEAD MEN LIE

Barcroft Boake

Out on the wastes of the Never Never —
  That's where the dead men lie!
There where the heat-waves dance for ever —
  That's where the dead men lie!
That's where the Earth's loved sons are keeping
Endless Tryst: not the west wind sweeping
Feverish pinions can wake their sleeping —
  Out where the dead men lie!

Where brown Summer and Death have mated —
  That's where the dead men lie!
Loving with fiery lust unsated —
  That's where the dead men lie!
Out where the grinning skulls bleach whitely
Under the saltbush sparkling brightly;
Out where the wild dogs chorus nightly —
  That's where the dead men lie!

Deep in the yellow, flowing river —
  That's where the dead men lie!
Under the banks where the shadows quiver —
  That's where the dead men lie!

[Where the platypus . . .

Where the platypus twists and doubles,
Leaving a train of tiny bubbles;
Rid at last of their earthly troubles —
  That's where the dead men lie!

East and backward pale faces turning —
  That's how the dead men lie!
Gaunt arms stretched with a voiceless yearning —
  That's how the dead men lie!
Oft in the fragrant hush of nooning
Hearing again their mother's crooning,
Wrapt for aye in a dreamful swooning —
  That's how the dead men lie!

Only the hand of Night can free them —
  That's when the dead men fly!
Only the frightened cattle see them —
  See the dead men go by!
Cloven hoofs beating out one measure,
Bidding the stockmen know no leisure —
That's when the dead men take their pleasure!
  That's when the dead men fly!

Ask, too, the never-sleeping drover:
  He sees the dead pass by;
Hearing them call to their friends — the plover,
  Hearing the dead men cry;
Seeing their faces stealing, stealing,
Hearing their laughter, pealing, pealing,
Watching their grey forms wheeling, wheeling
  Round where the cattle lie!

Strangled by thirst and fierce privation —
  That's how the dead men die!
Out on Moneygrub's farthest station —
  That's how the dead men die!
Hard-faced greybeards, youngsters callow;

Some mounds cared for, some left fallow;
Some deep down, yet others shallow;
  Some having but the sky.

Moneygrub, as he sips his claret,
  Looks with complacent eye
Down at his watch-chain, eighteen carat —
  There, in his club, hard by:
Recks not that every link is stamped with
Names of men whose limbs are cramped with
Too long lying in grave-mould, cramped with
  Death where the dead men lie.

TRUE PATRIOTS ALL

George Carter

From distant climes, o'er widespread seas we come,
Though not with much *eclat*, or beat of drum;
True patriots all, for be it understood,
We left our country for our country's good:
No private views disgraced our generous zeal,
What urged our travels was our country's weal:
And none will doubt but that our emigration
Has proved most useful to the British nation.

THE LAST OF HIS TRIBE

Henry Kendall

He crouches, and buries his face on his knees,
  And hides in the dark of his hair;
For he cannot look up to the storm-smitten trees,
  Or think of the loneliness there —
  Of the loss and the loneliness there.

The wallaroos grope through the tufts of the grass,
  And turn to their coverts for fear;
But he sits in the ashes and lets them pass
  Where the boomerangs sleep with the spear —
  With the nullah, the sling, and the spear.

Uloola, behold him! The thunder that breaks
  On the tops of the rocks with the rain,
And the wind which drives up with the salt of the lakes
  Have made him a hunter again —
  A hunter and fisher again.

For his eyes have been full with a smouldering thought;
  But he dreams of the hunts of yore,
And of foes that he sought, and of fights that he fought
  With those who will battle no more —
  Who will go to the battle no more.

It is well that the water which tumbles and fills,
  Goes moaning and moaning along;
For an echo rolls out from the sides of the hills,
  And he starts at a wonderful song —
  At the sound of a wonderful song.

And he sees, through the rents of the scattering fogs,
  The corroboree warlike and grim,

And the lubra who sat by the fire on the logs,
  To watch, like a mourner, for him —
  Like a mother and mourner for him.

Will he go in his sleep from these desolate lands,
  Like a chief, to the rest of his race,
With the honey-voiced woman who beckons and stands,
  And gleams like a dream in his face —
  Like a marvellous dream in his face?

THE BLUE MOUNTAINS

Henry Lawson

Above the ashes straight and tall,
  Through ferns with moisture dripping,
I climb beneath the sandstone wall,
  My feet on mosses slipping.

Like ramparts round the valley's edge
  The tinted cliffs are standing,
With many a broken wall and ledge,
  And many a rocky landing.

And round about their rugged feet
  Deep ferny dells are hidden
In shadowed depths, whence dust and heat
  Are banished and forbidden.

The stream that, crooning to itself,
  Comes down a tireless rover,

[Flows calmly to . . .

Flows calmly to the rocky shelf,
   And there leaps bravely over.

Now pouring down, now lost in spray
   When mountain breezes sally,
The water strikes the rock midway,
   And leaps into the valley.

Now in the west the colours change,
   The blue with crimson blending;
Behind the far Dividing Range
   The sun is fast descending.

And mellowed day comes o'er the place,
   And softens ragged edges;
The rising moon's great placid face
   Looks gravely o'er the ledges.

SAID HANRAHAN

P. J. Hartigan
("John O'Brien")

"We'll all be rooned," said Hanrahan
   In accents most forlorn
Outside the church ere Mass began
   One frosty Sunday morn.

The congregation stood about,
   Coat-collars to the ears,
And talked of stock and crops and drought
   As it had done for years.

"It's lookin' crook," said Daniel Croke;
  "Bedad, it's cruke, me lad,
For never since the banks went broke
  Has seasons been so bad."

"It's dry, all right," said young O'Neil,
  With which astute remark
He squatted down upon his heel
  And chewed a piece of bark.

And so around the chorus ran,
  "It's keepin' dry, no doubt."
"We'll all be rooned," said Hanrahan,
  "Before the year is out.

"The crops are done; ye'll have your work
  To save one bag of grain;
From here way out to Back-o'-Bourke
  They're singin' out for rain.

"They're singin' out for rain," he said,
  "And all the tanks are dry."
The congregation scratched its head.
  And gazed around the sky.

"There won't be grass, in any case,
  Enough to feed an ass;
There's not a blade on Casey's place
  As I came down to Mass."

"If rain don't come this month," said Dan,
  And cleared his throat to speak —
"We'll all be rooned," said Hanrahan,
  "If rain don't come this week."

[A heavy silence . . .

A heavy silence seemed to steal
On all at this remark;
And each man squatted on his heel,
And chewed a piece of bark.

"We want an inch of rain, we do,"
O'Neil observed at last;
But Croke "maintained" we wanted two
To put the danger past.

"If we don't get three inches, man,
Or four to break this drought,
We'll all be rooned," said Hanrahan,
"Before the year is out."

In God's good time down came the rain;
And all the afternoon
On iron roof and window-pane
It drummed a homely tune.

And through the night it pattered still,
And lightsome, gladsome elves
On dripping spout and window-sill
Kept talking to themselves.

It pelted, pelted all day long,
A-singing at its work,
Till every heart took up the song
Way out to Back-o'-Bourke.

And every creek a banker ran,
And dams filled overtop;
"We'll all be rooned," said Hanrahan,
"If this rain doesn't stop."

And stop it did, in God's good time:
  And spring came in to fold
A mantle o'er the hills sublime
  Of green and pink and gold.

And days went by on dancing feet,
  With harvest-hopes immense,
And laughing eyes beheld the wheat
  Nid-nodding o'er the fence.

And, oh, the smiles on every face,
  As happy lad and lass
Through grass knee-deep in Casey's place
  Went riding down to Mass.

While round the church in clothes genteel
  Discoursed the men of mark,
And each man squatted on his heel,
  And chewed his piece of bark.

"There'll be bush-fires for sure, me man,
  There will, without a doubt;
We'll all be rooned," said Hanrahan,
  "Before the year is out."

THE MAN FROM SNOWY RIVER

A. B. ("Banjo") Paterson

There was movement at the station, for the word had passed around
That the colt from old Regret had got away,
And had joined the wild bush horses — he was worth a thousand pound,
So all the cracks had gathered to the fray.
All the tried and noted riders from the stations near and far
Had mustered at the homestead overnight,
For the bushmen love hard riding where the wild bush horses are,
And the stock-horse snuffs the battle with delight.

There was Harrison, who made his pile when Pardon won the cup,
The old man with his hair as white as snow;
But few could ride beside him when his blood was fairly up —
He would go wherever horse and man could go.
And Clancy of the Overflow came down to lend a hand,
No better horseman ever held the reins;
For never horse could throw him while the saddle-girths would stand —
He learnt to ride while droving on the plains.

And one was there, a stripling on a small and weedy beast;
He was something like a racehorse undersized,
With a touch of Timor pony — three parts thoroughbred at least —
And such as are by mountain horsemen prized.
He was hard and tough and wiry — just the sort that won't say die —
There was courage in his quick impatient tread;
And he bore the badge of gameness in his bright and fiery eye,
And the proud and lofty carriage of his head.

But still so slight and weedy, one would doubt his power to stay,
And the old man said, "That horse will never do
For a long and tiring gallop — lad, you'd better stop away,

[Those hills are far . . .

Those hills are far too rough for such as you."
So he waited, sad and wistful — only Clancy stood his friend —
"I think we ought to let him come," he said;
"I warrant he'll be with us when he's wanted at the end,
For both his horse and he are mountain bred.

"He hails from Snowy River, up by Kosciusko's side,
Where the hills are twice as steep and twice as rough;
Where a horse's hoofs strike firelight from the flint stones every stride,
The man that holds his own is good enough.
And the Snowy River riders on the mountains make their home,
Where the river runs those giant hills between;
I have seen full many horsemen since I first commenced to roam,
But nowhere yet such horsemen have I seen."

So he went; they found the horses by the big mimosa clump,
They raced away towards the mountain's brow,
And the old man gave his orders, "Boys, go at them from the jump,
No use to try for fancy riding now.
And, Clancy, you must wheel them, try and wheel them to the right.
Ride boldly, lad, and never fear the spills,
For never yet was rider that could keep the mob in sight,
If once they gain the shelter of those hills."

So Clancy rode to wheel them — he was racing on the wing
Where the best and boldest riders take their place,
And he raced his stock-horse past them, and he made the ranges ring
With the stockwhip, as he met them face to face.
Then they halted for a moment, while he swung the dreaded lash,
But they saw their well-loved mountains full in view,
And they charged beneath the stockwhip with a sharp and sudden dash,
And off into the mountain scrub they flew.

Then fast the horsemen followed, where the gorges deep and black
Resounded to the thunder of their tread,
And the stockwhips woke the echoes, and they fiercely answered back
From cliffs and crags that beetled overhead.

And upward, ever upward, the wild horses held their way,
Where mountain ash and kurrajong grew wide;
And the old man muttered fiercely, "We may bid the mob good day,
No man can hold them down the other side."

When they reached the mountain's summit, even Clancy took a pull —
It well might make the boldest hold their breath;
The wild hop scrub grew thickly, and the hidden ground was full
Of wombat holes, and any slip was death.
But the man from Snowy River let the pony have his head,
And he swung his stockwhip round and gave a cheer,
And he raced him down the mountain like a torrent down its bed,
While the others stood and watched in very fear.

He sent the flint stones flying, but the pony kept his feet,
He cleared the fallen timber in his stride,
And the man from Snowy River never shifted in his seat —
It was grand to see that mountain horseman ride.
Through the stringy-barks and saplings, on the rough and broken ground,
Down the hillside at a racing pace he went;
And he never drew the bridle till he landed safe and sound
At the bottom of that terrible descent.

He was right among the horses as they climbed the farther hill,
And the watchers on the mountain, standing mute,
Saw him ply the stockwhip fiercely; he was right among them still,
As he raced across the clearing in pursuit.
Then they lost him for a moment, where two mountain gullies met
In the ranges — but a final glimpse reveals
On a dim and distant hillside the wild horses racing yet,
With the man from Snowy River at their heels.

And he ran them single-handed till their sides were white with foam;
He followed like a bloodhound on their track,
Till they halted, cowed and beaten; then he turned their heads for home,

[And alone and unassisted . . .

And alone and unassisted brought them back.
But his hardy mountain pony he could scarcely raise a trot,
He was blood from hip to shoulder from the spur;
But his pluck was still undaunted, and his courage fiery hot,
For never yet was mountain horse a cur.

And down by Kosciusko, where the pine-clad ridges raise
Their torn and rugged battlements on high,
Where the air is clear as crystal, and the white stars fairly blaze
At midnight in the cold and frosty sky,
And where around the Overflow the reed-beds sweep and sway
To the breezes, and the rolling plains are wide,
The Man from Snowy River is a household word today,
And the stockmen tell the story of his ride.

OUR CORRUGATED-IRON TANK

Hal Gye
("James Hackston")

Our tank stood on a crazy stand,
Bare to the burning sky,
White-hot as glares the desert sand,
And dismal to the eye.
Its lid was like a rakish hat,
The tap bent all awry
And with a drip so constant that
It almost dripped when dry.

It was a most convenient tank
Wherein most things could fall;

Where snakes came from the bush and drank,
The rabbits used to call,
The mice committed suicide,
The gum-leaves sank to rest,
And in it possums dropped and died
And hornets made their nest.

But stark within my memory
I see it once again
When we looked at it anxiously —
Days when we hoped for rain;
I hear the hollow sounds it made,
Like some prophetic drum,
As I tapped rung on rung, afraid
Of dreadful days to come,
When mother in despair would pray
As low the water sank:
Four rungs, three rungs, two rungs, and, aye,
How miserly we drank;
And there was none for face or hands,
Waste was a wicked thing,
There in the baked and parching lands,
With hope our only spring.

Next came the fatal "One rung left!"
(How cruel words can be!)
As we all stood for joys bereft,
Dumb in our misery:
And then I tapped the tank in pain —
Those knells of drought and doom:
Our tank at last gone dry again,
Our home cast down in gloom;

But, oh, the joy that filled our hearts
When came the bounteous rain

[And the drain-pipe sang . . .

And the drain-pipe sang in fits and starts
And filled the tank again!
We felt as if we'd riches won,
That life again was sweet;
And overjoyed then, everyone,
We even washed our feet!

THE TRAVELLER

C. J. Dennis

As I rode in to Burrumbeet,
I met a man with funny feet;
And, when I paused to ask him why
His feet were strange, he rolled his eye
And said the rain would spoil the wheat;
So I rode on to Burrumbeet.

As I rode in to Beetaloo,
I met a man whose nose was blue;
And, when I asked him how he got
A nose like that, he answered, "What
Do bullocks mean when they say 'Moo'?"
So I rode on to Beetaloo.

As I rode in to Ballarat,
I met a man who wore no hat;
And, when I said he might take cold,
He cried, "The hills are quite as old
As yonder plains, but not so flat."
So I rode on to Ballarat.

As I rode in to Gundagai,
I met a man and passed him by
Without a nod, without a word.
He turned, and said he'd never heard
Or seen a man so wise as I.
But I rode on to Gundagai.

As I rode homeward, full of doubt,
I met a stranger riding out:
A foolish man he seemed to me;
But, "Nay, I am yourself," said he,
"Just as you were when you rode out."
So I rode homeward, free of doubt.

SEPTEMBER IN AUSTRALIA

Henry Kendall

Grey winter hath gone, like a wearisome guest,
  And behold, for repayment,
September comes in with the wind of the west
  And the Spring in her raiment!
The ways of the frost have been filled of the flowers,
  While the forest discovers
Wild wings, with a halo of hyaline hours,
  And the music of lovers.

September the maid with the swift, silver feet!
  She glides, and she graces
The valleys of coolness, the slopes of the heat,

[With her blossomy . . .

With her blossomy traces;
Sweet month, with a mouth that is made of a rose,
She lightens and lingers
In spots where the harp of the evening glows,
Attuned by her fingers.

High places that knew of the gold and the white
On the forehead of Morning
Now darken and quake, and the steps of the Night
Are heavy with warning.
Her voice in the distance is lofty and loud
Through the echoing gorges;
She hath hidden her eyes in a mantle of cloud,
And her feet in the surges.

On the tops of the hills, on the turreted cones —
Chief temples of thunder —
The gale, like a ghost, in the middle watch moans.
Gliding over and under.
The sea, flying white through the rack and the rain,
Leapeth wild at the forelands;
And the plover, whose cry is like passion with pain,
Complains in the moorlands.

Oh, season of changes — of shadow and shine —
September the splendid!
My song hath no music to mingle with thine,
And its burden is ended;
But thou, being born of the winds and the sun.
By mountain, by river,
Mayst lighten and listen, and loiter and run,
With thy voices for ever!

NATIVE-BORN

Eve Langley

In a white gully among fungus red
  Where serpent logs lay hissing at the air,
I found a kangaroo. Tall, dewy, dead,
  So like a woman, she lay silent there.
Her ivory hands, black-nailed, crossed on her breast,
  Her skin of sun and moon hues, fallen cold.
Her brown eyes lay like rivers come to rest
  And death had made her black mouth harsh and old.
Beside her in the ashes I sat deep
  And mourned for her, but had no native song
To flatter death, while down the ploughlands steep
  Dark young Camelli whistled loud and long,
"Love, liberty, and Italy are all."
  Broad golden was his breast against the sun.
I saw his wattle whip rise high and fall
  Across the slim mare's flanks, and one by one
She drew the furrows after her as he
  Flapped like a gull behind her, climbing high,
Chanting his oaths and lashing soundingly,
  While from the mare came once a blowing sigh.
The dew upon the kangaroo's white side
  Had melted. Time was whirling high around,
Like the thin woomera, and from heaven wide
  He, the bull-roarer, made continuous sound.
Incarnate lay my country by my hand:
  Her long hot days, bushfires, and speaking rains,
Her mornings of opal and the copper band
  Of smoke around the sunlight on the plains.
Globed in fire-bodies the meat-ants ran
  To taste her flesh and linked us as we lay,

[For ever Australian . . .

For ever Australian, listening to a man
  From careless Italy, swearing at our day.
When, golden-lipped, the eagle-hawks came down
  Hissing and whistling to eat of lovely her,
And the blowflies with their shields of purple brown
  Plied hatching to and fro across her fur,
I burnt her with the logs, and stood all day
  Among the ashes, pressing home the flame
Till woman, logs, and dreams were scorched away,
  And native with night, that land from whence they came.

BELL-BIRDS

Henry Kendall

By channels of coolness the echoes are calling,
And down the dim gorges I hear the creek falling;
It lives in the mountain, where moss and the sedges
Touch with their beauty the banks and the ledges:
Through breaks of the cedar and sycamore bowers
Struggles the light that is love to the flowers.
And softer than slumber, and sweeter than singing,
The notes of the bell-birds are running and ringing.

The silver-voiced bell-birds, the darlings of day-time,
They sing in September their songs of the May-time.
When shadows wax strong, and the thunder-bolts hurtle,
They hide with their fear in the leaves of the myrtle;
When rain and the sunbeams shine mingled together,
They start up like fairies that follow fair weather,
And straightway the hues of the feathers unfolden
Are the green and the purple, the blue and the golden.

October, the maiden of bright yellow tresses,
Loiters for love in these cool wildernesses;
Loiters knee-deep in the grasses to listen,
Where dripping rocks gleam and the leafy pools glisten.
Then is the time when the water-moons splendid
Break with their gold, and are scattered or blended
Over the creeks, till the woodlands have warning
Of songs of the bell-bird and wings of the morning.

Welcome as waters unkissed by the summers
Are the voices of bell-birds to thirsty far-comers.
When fiery December sets foot in the forest,
And the need of the wayfarer presses the sorest,
Pent in the ridges for ever and ever,
The bell-birds direct him to spring and to river,
With ring and with ripple, like runnels whose torrents
Are toned by the pebbles and leaves in the currents.

Often I sit, looking back to a childhood
Mixt with the sights and the sounds of the wildwood,
Longing for power and the sweetness to fashion
Lyrics with beats like the heart-beats of passion —
Songs interwoven of lights and of laughters
Borrowed from bell-birds in far forest rafters;
So I might keep in the city and alleys
The beauty and strength of the deep mountain valleys,
Charming to slumber the pain of my losses
With glimpses of creeks and a vision of mosses.

THE TEAMS

Henry Lawson

A cloud of dust on the long, white road,
  And the teams go creeping on
Inch by inch with the weary load;
And by the power of the green-hide goad
  The distant goal is won.

With eyes half-shut to the blinding dust,
  And necks to the yokes bent low,
The beasts are pulling as bullocks must;
And the shining tires might almost rust
  While the spokes are turning slow.

With face half-hid by a broad-brimmed hat,
  That shades from the heat's white waves,
And shouldered whip, with its green-hide plait,
The driver plods with a gait like that
  Of his weary, patient slaves.

He wipes his brow, for the day is hot,
  And spits to the left with spite;
He shouts at Bally, and flicks at Scot,
And raises dust from the back of Spot,
  And spits to the dusty right.

He'll sometimes pause as a thing of form
  In front of a settler's door,
And ask for a drink, and remark "It's warm".
Or say "There's signs of a thunderstorm";
  But he seldom utters more.

[The rains are heavy . . .

The rains are heavy on roads like these
  And, fronting his lonely home,
For days together the settler sees
The waggons bogged to the axletrees,
  Or ploughing the sodden loam.

And then, when the roads are at their worst,
  The bushman's children hear
The cruel blows of the whips reversed
While bullocks pull as their hearts would burst,
  And bellow with pain and fear.

And thus — with glimpses of home and rest —
  Are the long, long journeys done;
And thus — 'tis a thankless life at the best! —
Is Distance fought in the mighty West,
  And the lonely battle won.

NINE MILES FROM GUNDAGAI

Jack Moses

I've done my share of shearing sheep,
Of droving and all that,
And bogged a bullock-team as well,
On a Murrumbidgee flat.
I've seen the bullock stretch and strain,
And blink his bleary eye,
And the dog sit on the tucker box,
Nine miles from Gundagai.

I've been jilted, jarred, and crossed in love,
And sand-bagged in the dark,
Till if a mountain fell on me
I'd treat it as a lark.
It's when you've got your bullocks bogged
That's the time you flog and cry,
And the dog sits on the tucker box,
Nine miles from Gundagai.

We've all got our little troubles,
In life's hard, thorny way.
Some strike them in a motor car
And others in a dray.
But when your dog and bullocks strike
It ain't no apple pie,
And the dog sat on the tucker box
Nine miles from Gundagai.

But that's all past and dead and gone,
And I've sold the team for meat,
And perhaps some day where I was bogged,
There'll be an asphalt street.
The dog, ah! well he got a bait,
And thought he'd like to die,
So I buried him in the tucker box,
Nine miles from Gundagai.

THE HALL OF
COMMERCE.
RYAN & INSON'S.
Hall of

COUNTRY TOWNS

Kenneth Slessor

Country towns, with your willows and squares,
And farmers bouncing on barrel mares
To public-houses of yellow wood
With "1860" over their doors,
And that mysterious race of Hogans
Which always keeps General Stores . . .

At the School of Arts, a broadsheet lies
Sprayed with the sarcasm of flies:
"The Great Golightly Family
Of Entertainers Here To-night" —
Dated a year and a half ago,
But left there, less from carelessness
Than from a wish to seem polite.

Verandas baked with musky sleep,
Mulberry faces dozing deep,
And dogs that lick the sunlight up
Like paste of gold — or, roused in vain
By far, mysterious buggy-wheels,
Lower their ears, and drowse again . . .

Country towns with your schooner bees,
And locusts burnt in the pepper-trees,
Drown me with syrups, arch your boughs,
Find me a bench, and let me snore,
Till, charged with ale and unconcern,
I'll think it's noon at half-past four!

DAYS WHEN WE WENT SWIMMING

Henry Lawson

The breezes waved the silver grass
  Waist-high along the siding,
And to the creek we ne'er could pass,
  Three boys, on bare back riding;
Beneath the sheoaks in the bend
  The waterhole was brimming —
Do you remember yet, old friend,
  The times we went in swimming?

The days we played the wag from school —
  Joys shared — but paid for singly —
The air was hot, the water cool —
  And naked boys are kingly!
With mud for soap, the sun to dry —
  A well-planned lie to stay us,
And dust well rubbed on neck and face
  Lest cleanliness betray us.

And you'll remember farmer Kutz —
  Though scarcely for his bounty —
He'd leased a forty-acre block,
  And thought he owned the county;
A farmer of the old-world school,
  That men grew hard and grim in,
He drew his water from the pool
  That we preferred to swim in.

And do you mind when down the creek
  His angry way he wended,
A green-hide cartwhip in his hand

[For our young backs . . .

For our young backs intended?
Three naked boys upon the sand —
Half-buried and half-sunning
Three startled boys without their clothes
Across the paddocks running.

We'd had some scares, but we looked blank
When, resting there and chumming,
We glanced by chance along the bank
And saw the farmer coming!
Some home impressions linger yet
Of cups of sorrow brimming;
I hardly think that we'll forget
The last day we went swimming.

AUSTRALIA

A. D. Hope

A nation of trees, drab green and desolate grey
In the field uniform of modern wars
Darkens her hills, those endless, outstretched paws
Of Sphinx demolished or stone lion worn away.

They call her a young country, but they lie:
She is the last of lands, the emptiest,
A woman beyond her change of life, a breast
Still tender but within the womb is dry.

Without songs, architecture, history:
The emotions and superstitions of younger lands,
Her rivers of water drawn among inland sands,
The river of her immense stupidity

Floods her monotonous tribes from Cairns to Perth.
In them at last the ultimate men arrive
Whose boast is not: "we live" but "we survive"
A type who will inhabit the dying earth.

And her five cities, like five teeming sores
Each drains her, a vast parasite robber-state
Where second-hand Europeans pullulate
Timidly on the edge of alien shores.

Yet there are some like me turn gladly home
From the lush jungle of modern thought, to find
The Arabian desert of the human mind,
Hoping, if still from the deserts the prophets come,

Such savage and scarlet as no green hills dare
Springs in that waste, some spirit which escapes
The learned doubt, the chatter of cultured apes
Which is called civilization over there.

I SAW THE BEAUTY GO

Mary Gilmore

I saw the beauty go,
The beauty that, in a stream,
Flowed through the breadth of the land
Like the fenceless foot of a dream.

There went the kangaroos, that, in hosts,
For their bedding-down grouped at even,
Only the sound of the nibbling lips
Making the sunset steven.

Then as they stilled, and the moon
With her white cloths mantled the trees,
From the shadows beneath the mopoke called,
And the curlew made her pleas.

I saw the beauty go,
The beauty that could not be tamed;
But before it went it looked at me
With the eyes of the maimed.

IN A SOUTHERN GARDEN

Dorothea Mackellar

When the tall bamboos are clicking to the restless little breeze,
And bats begin their jerky skimming flight,
And the creamy scented blossoms of the dark pittosporum trees,
Grow sweeter with the coming of the night.

And the harbour in the distance lies beneath a purple pall,
And nearer, at the garden's lowest fringe,
Loud the water soughs and gurgles 'mid the rocks below the wall,
Dark-heaving with a dim uncanny tinge

Of a green as pale as beryls, like the strange faint-coloured flame
That burns around the Women of the Sea:
And the strip of sky to westward which the camphor-laurels frame,
Has turned to ash-of-rose and ivory —

And a chorus rises valiantly from where the crickets hide,
Close-shaded by the balsams drooping down —
It is evening in a garden by the kindly waterside,
A garden near the lights of Sydney town!

SHEARING IN THE BAR

H. P. ("Duke") Tritton

My shearing days are over, though I never was a gun:
I could always count my twenty at the end of every run.
I used the old Trade Union shears, and the blades were running full
As I shoved them to the knockers and I pushed away the wool.
I shore at Goorianawa and never got the sack;
From Breeza out to Comprador I always could go back;
But though I am a truthful man I find, when in a bar,
That my tally's always doubled but — I never call for tar!

Now shearing on the Western Plains, where the fleece is full of sand
And clover-burr and cork-screw grass, is the place to try your hand;
For the sheep are tough and wiry where they feed on the Mitchell Grass,
And every second one of them is close to the "cobbler" class;
And a pen chocked full of "cobblers" is a shearer's dream of hell,
And loud and lurid are their words when they catch one on the bell:
But when we're pouring down the grog you'll hear no call for tar,
For the shearer never cuts them — when he's shearing in a bar!

At Louth I got the bell-sheep, a wrinkly tough-woolled brute,
Who never stopped his kicking till I tossed him down the 'chute.
Though my wrist was aching badly, I fought him all the way:
I couldn't afford to miss a blow — I must earn my pound a day;
So when I took a strip of skin, I would hide it with my knee —
Gently turn the sheep around so the right bower couldn't see,
Then try to catch the rousy's eye, and softly whisper, "Tar";
But it never seems to happen — when I'm shearing in a bar!

I shore away the belly-wool, and trimmed the crutch and hocks,
Then opened up along the neck, while the rousy swept the locks,
Then smartly swung the sheep around, and dumped him on his rear —

[Two blows to chip away . . .

Two blows to chip away the wig — (I also took an ear!)
Then down around the shoulder and the blades were opened wide,
As I drove them on the long blow and down the whipping side;
And when I tossed him down the 'chute he was nearly black with tar,
But it never seems to happen — when I'm shearing at the bar!

Now when the season's ended and my grandsons all come back
In their *Vanguards* and their *Holdens* — I was always "on the track" —
They come and take me into town to fill me up with beer,
And I sit on a corner-stool and listen to them shear:
There's not a bit of difference! It must make the angels weep,
To hear a mob of shearers in a bar-room shearing sheep;
The sheep go rattling down the race and there's never a call for tar,
For they still don't seem to cut them — when they're shearing in a bar!

Then memories come crowding and they roll away the years,
And my hands begin to tighten and they seem to feel the shears:
I want to tell them of the sheds, of sheds where I have shorn,
Full fifty years, or maybe more, before the boys were born.
I want to speak of Yarragreen, Dunlop or Wingadee,
But the beer has started working and I find I cannot see.
So I'd better not start shearing — I'd be bound to call for tar;
Then be treated like a blackleg — when I'm shearing in a bar!

HOW M'DOUGALL TOPPED THE SCORE

Thomas E. Spencer

A peaceful spot is Piper's Flat. The folks that live around,
They keep themselves by keeping sheep and turning up the ground.
But the climate is erratic; and the consequences are
The struggle with the elements is everlasting war.
We plough, and sow, and harrow — then sit down and pray for rain;
And then we all get flooded out, and have to start again.
But the folks are now rejoicing as they ne'er rejoiced before,
For we've played Molongo cricket, and M'Dougall topped the score!

Molongo had a head on it, and challenged us to play
A single-innings match for lunch — the losing team to pay.
We were not great guns at cricket, but we couldn't well say *No*,
So we all began to practice, and we let the reaping go.
We scoured the flat for ten miles round to muster up our men,
But when the list was totalled we could only number ten.
Then up spoke big Tim Brady, he was always slow to speak,
And he said — "What price M'Dougall, who lives down at Cooper's Creek?"

So we sent of old M'Dougall, and he stated in reply
That he'd never played at cricket, but he'd half a mind to try.
He couldn't come to practice — he was getting in his hay,
But he guessed he'd show the beggars from Molongo how to play.
Now M'Dougall was a Scotchman, and a canny one at that,
So he started in to practice with a paling for a bat.
He got Mrs Mac. to bowl him, but she couldn't run at all,
So he trained his sheep dog, Pincher, how to scout and fetch the ball.

Now, Pincher was no puppy; he was old, and worn and grey;
But he understood M'Dougall, and — accustomed to obey —
When M'Dougall cried out "Fetch it!" he would fetch it in a trice;

[But until the word . . .

But until the word was "Drop it!" he would grip it like a vice.
And each succeeding night they played until the light grew dim;
Sometimes M'Dougall struck the ball — sometimes the ball struck *him*!
Each time he struck, the ball would plough a furrow in the ground,
And when he missed, the impetus would turn him three times round.

The fatal day at length arrived — the day that was to see
Molongo bite the dust, or Piper's Flat knocked up a tree!
Molongo's captain won the toss, and sent his men to bat,
And they gave some leather-hunting to the men of Piper's Flat.
When the ball sped where M'Dougall stood, firm planted in its track,
He shut his eyes, and turned him round, and stopped it — with his *back*!
The highest score was twenty-two, the total sixty-six,
When Brady sent a yorker down that scattered Johnson's sticks.

Then Piper's Flat went in to bat, for glory and renown,
But, like to grass before the scythe, our wickets tumbled down.
"Nine wickets down for seventeen, with fifty more to win!"
Our captain heaved a heavy sigh — and sent M'Dougall in.
"Ten pounds to one you lose it!" cried a barracker from town;
But M'Dougall said "I'll tak' it, mon!" and planked the money down.
Then he girded up his moleskins in a self-reliant style,
Threw off his hat and boots, and faced the bowler with a smile.

He held the bat the wrong side out, and Johnson with a grin,
Stepped lightly to the bowling crease, and sent a "wobbler" in;
M'Dougall spooned it softly back, and Johnson waited there,
But M'Dougall, crying "*Fetch it*!" started running like a hare.
Molongo shouted "Victory! He's out as sure as eggs,"
When Pincher started through the crowd, and ran through Johnson's legs.
He seized the ball like lightning; then he ran behind a log.
And M'Dougall kept on running, while Molongo chased the dog.

They chased him up, they chased him down, they chased him round, and the
He darted through a slip-rail as the scorer shouted "Ten!"
M'Dougall puffed; Molongo swore; excitement was intense;
As the scorer marked down "Twenty," Pincher cleared a barbed-wire fence.

"Let us head him!" shrieked Molongo. "Brain the mongrel with a bat!"
"Run it out! Good old M'Dougall!" yelled the men of Piper's Flat.
And M'Dougall kept on jogging, and then Pincher doubled back,
And the scorer counted "*Forty*" as they raced across the track.

M'Dougall's legs were going fast, Molongo's breath was gone —
But while Molongo chased the dog — M'Dougall struggled on.
When the scorer shouted "*Fifty*!" then they knew the chase could cease.
And M'Dougall gasped out "Drop it!" as he dropped within his crease.
Then Pincher dropped the ball, and, as instinctively he knew
Discretion was the wiser plan, he disappeared from view.
And as Molongo's beaten men exhausted lay around,
We raised M'Dougall shoulder-high, and bore him from the ground.

We bore him to M'Ginnis's, where lunch was ready laid,
And filled him up with whisky-punch, for which Molongo paid.
We drank his health in bumpers, and we cheered him three times three,
And when Molongo got its breath, Molongo joined the spree.
And the critics say they never saw a cricket match like that,
When M'Dougall broke the record in the game at Piper's Flat.
And the folk are jubilating as they never were before;
For we played Molongo cricket, and *M'Dougall topped the score.*

THE DEATH OF BEN HALL

Will H. Ogilvie

Ben Hall was out on the Lachlan side
With a thousand pounds on his head;
A score of troopers were scattered wide
And a hundred more were ready to ride
Wherever a rumour led.

They had followed his track from the Weddin heights
And north by the Weelong yards;
Through dazzling days and moonlit nights
They had sought him over their rifle-sights,
With their hands on their trigger-guards.

The outlaw stole like a hunted fox
Through the scrub and stunted heath,
And peered like a hawk from his eyrie rocks
Through the wave boughs of the sapling box
On the troopers riding beneath.

His clothes were rent by the clutching thorn
And his blistered feet were bare;
Ragged and torn, with his beard unshorn,
He hid in the woods like a beast forlorn,
With a padded path to his lair.

But every night when the white stars rose
He crossed by the Gunning Plain
To a stockman's hut where the Gunning flows,
And struck on the door three swift light blows,
And a hand unhooked the chain —

And the outlaw followed the lone path back
With food for another day;

And the kindly darkness covered his track
And the shadows swallowed him deep and black
Where the starlight melted away.

But his friend had read of the Big Reward,
And his soul was stirred with greed;
He fastened his door and window-board,
He saddled his horse and crossed the ford,
And spurred to the town at speed.

You may ride at a man's or a maid's behest
When honour or true love call
And steel your heart to the worst or best,
But the ride that is ta'en on a traitor's quest
Is the bitterest ride of all.

A hot wind blew from the Lachlan bank
And a curse on its shoulder came;
The pine-trees frowned at him, rank on rank,
The sun on a gathering storm-cloud sank
And flushed his cheek with shame.

He reined at the Court; and the tale began
That the rifles alone should end;
Sergeant and trooper laid their plan
To draw the net on a hunted man
At the treacherous word of a friend.

False was the hand that raised the chain
And false was the whispered word:
"The troopers have turned to the south again,
You may care to camp on the Gunning Plain."
And the weary outlaw heard.

He walked from the hut but a quarter-mile

[Where a clump . . .

Where a clump of saplings stood
In a sea of grass like a lonely isle;
And a moon came up in a little while
Like silver steeped in blood.

Ben Hall lay down on the dew-wet ground
By the side of his tiny fire;
And a night-breeze woke, and he heard no sound
As the troopers drew their cordon round —
And the traitor earned his hire.

And nothing they saw in the dim grey light,
But the little glow in the trees;
And they crouched in the tall cold grass all night,
Each one ready to shoot at sight,
With his rifle cocked on his knees.

When the shadows broke and the dawn's white sword
Swung over the mountain wall,
And a little wind blew over the ford,
A sergeant sprang to his feet and roared:
"In the name of the Queen, Ben Hall!"

Haggard, the outlaw leapt from his bed
With his lean arms held on high.
"Fire!" And the word was scarcely said
When the mountains rang to a rain of lead —
And the dawn went drifting by.

They kept their word and they paid his pay
Where a clean man's hand would shrink;
And that was the traitor's master-day
As he stood by the bar on his homeward way
And called on the crowd to drink.

He banned no creed and he barred no class,
And he called to his friends by name;

But the worst would shake his head and pass
And none would drink from the bloodstained glass
And the goblet red with shame.

And I know when I hear the last grim call
And my mortal hour is spent,
When the light is hid and the curtains fall
I would rather sleep with the dead Ben Hall
Than go where that traitor went.

CONDAMINE BELLS

Jack Sorensen

By a forge near a hut on the Condamine River
  A blacksmith laboured at his ancient trade;
With his hammer swinging and his anvil ringing
  He fashioned bells from a crosscut blade.

And while he toiled by the Condamine River
  He sang a song for a job well done;
And the song and the clamour of his busy hammer
  Merged and mingled in a tempered tone.

And his bells rang clear from the Condamine River
  To the Gulf, to the Leeuwin, over soil and sand;
Desert eagles winging heard his stock-bells ringing
  As a first voice singing in a songless land.

The smith is lost to the Condamine River,
  Gone is the humpy where he used to dwell;
But the songs and the clamour of his busy hammer
  Ring on through the land in the Condamine Bell.

CLANCY OF THE OVERFLOW

A. B. ("Banjo") Paterson

I had written him a letter which I had, for want of better
  Knowledge, sent to where I met him down the Lachlan, years ago;
He was shearing when I knew him, so I sent the letter to him,
  Just on spec, addressed as follows, "Clancy of the Overflow."

And an answer came directed in a writing unexpected
  (And I think the same was written with a thumb-nail dipped in tar):
'Twas his shearing mate who wrote it, and *verbatim* I will quote it:
  "Clancy's gone to Queensland droving, and we don't know where he are."

In my wild erratic fancy visions come to me of Clancy
  Gone a-droving "down the Cooper" where the Western drovers go;
As the stock are slowly stringing, Clancy rides behind them singing,
  For the drover's life has pleasures that the townsfolk never know.

And the bush has friends to meet him, and their kindly voices greet him
  In the murmur of the breezes and the river on its bars,
And he sees the vision splendid of the sunlit plains extended,
  And at night the wondrous glory of the everlasting stars.

I am sitting in my dingy little office, where a stingy
  Ray of sunlight struggles feebly down between the houses tall,
And the foetid air and gritty of the dusty, dirty city,
  Through the open window floating, spreads its foulness over all.

And in place of lowing cattle, I can hear the fiendish rattle
  Of the tramways and the buses making hurry down the street;
And the language uninviting of the gutter children fighting
  Comes fitfully and faintly through the ceaseless tramp of feet.

[And the hurrying people . . .

And the hurrying people daunt me, and their pallid faces haunt me
  As they shoulder one another in their rush and nervous haste,
With their eager eyes and greedy, and their stunted forms and weedy,
  For townsfolk have no time to grow, they have no time to waste.

And I somehow rather fancy that I'd like to change with Clancy,
  Like to take a turn at droving where the seasons come and go,
While he faced the round eternal of the cash-book and the journal.—
  But I doubt he'd suit the office, Clancy of the Overflow.

STIRRUP SONG

Harry ("The Breaker") Morant

We've drunk our wine, we've kissed our girls, and funds are getting low,
The horses must be thinking it's a fair thing now to go.
Sling up the swags on Condamine, and strap the billies fast,
And stuff a bottle in the bag, and let's be off at last.

What matter if the creeks are up! — the cash, alas, runs down! —
A very sure and certain sign we're long enough in town;
The nigger rides the "boko", and you'd better take the bay,
Quartpot will do to carry me the stage we'll go today.

No grass this side the Border fence, and all the mulga's dead;
The horses for a day or two will have to spiel ahead;
Man never yet from Queensland brought a bullock or a hack
But lost condition on that God-abandoned Border track.

But once we're through the rabbit-proof, it's certain since the rain
There's whips of grass and water, so it's "West-by-North" again;
There's feed on Tyson's country, we can spell the mokes a week
Where Billy Stevens last year trapped his brumbies, on Bough Creek.

The Paroo may be quickly crossed — the Eulo Common's bare —
And anyhow it isn't wise, old man, to dally there!
Alack-a-day! far wiser men than you or I succumb
To woman's wiles and potency of Queensland wayside rum!

Then over sand and spinifex! and on o'er range and plain!
The nags are fresh; besides they know they're westward-bound again!
The brand upon old Darkie's thigh is that upon the hide
Of bullocks we shall muster on the Diamantina side.

We'll light our campfires while we may, and yarn beside the blaze,
The jingling hobble-chains shall make a music through the days;
And while the tucker-bags are right and we've a stock of weed
The swagman will be welcome to a pipeful and a feed.

So fill your pipe, and ere we mount we'll drain a parting nip:
Here's now that West-by-North again may prove a lucky trip;
Then back once more, let's trust you'll find your best girl's merry face,
Or, if she jilts you, may you get a better in her place!

CLICK GO THE SHEARS

Anon

Out on the board the old shearer stands,
Grasping his shears in his long, bony hands;
Fixed is his gaze on a bare-bellied yeo,
Glory if he gets her, won't he make the "ringer" go!

Chorus:
Click go the shears boys, click, click, click;
Wide is his blow and his hands move quick,
The ringer looks round and is beaten by a blow,
And curses the old snagger with the bare-bellied yeo.

In the middle of the floor, in his cane-bottomed chair
Is the boss of the board, with eyes everywhere;
Notes well each fleece as it comes to the screen,
Paying strict attention if it's taken off clean.

The colonial experience man, he is there, of course,
With his shiny leggin's, just got off his horse;
Casting round his eye, like a real connoisseur,
Whistling the old tune, "I'm the Perfect Lure."

The tar-boy is there, awaiting in demand,
With his blackened tar-pot, and his tarry hand,
Sees one old sheep with a cut upon its back,
Hears what he's waiting for, "Tar here, Jack!"

Shearing is all over and we've all got our cheques.
Roll up your swag boys, we're off on the tracks;
The first pub we come to, it's there we'll have a spree,
And everyone that comes along, it's "Have a drink with me!"

[Down by the bar . . .

Down by the bar the old shearer stands,
Grasping his glass in his thin bony hands;
Fixed is his gaze on a green-painted keg,
Glory, he'll get down on it, ere he stirs a peg.

There we leave him standing, shouting for all hands,
Whilst all around him, every drinker stands:
His eyes are on the cask, which is now lowering fast,
He works hard, he drinks hard, and goes to hell at last!

THE BUSH

James Lister Cuthbertson

Give us from dawn to dark
  Blue of Australian skies,
Let there be none to mark
  Whither our pathway lies.

Give us when noontide comes
  Rest in the woodland free —
Fragrant breath of the gums,
  Cold, sweet scent of the sea.

Give us the wattle's gold
  And the dew-laden air,
And the loveliness bold
  Loneliest landscapes wear.

These are the haunts we love,
  Glad with enchanted hours,
Bright as the heavens above,
  Fresh as the wild bush flowers.

ANDY'S GONE WITH CATTLE

Henry Lawson

Our Andy's gone with cattle now —
  Our hearts are out of order —
With drought he's gone to battle now
  Across the Queensland border.

He's left us in dejection now;
  Our thoughts with him are roving;
It's dull on this selection now,
  Since Andy went a-droving.

Who now shall wear the cheerful face
  In times when things are slackest?
And who shall whistle round the place
  When Fortune frowns her blackest?

Oh, who shall cheek the squatter now
  When he comes round us snarling?
His tongue is growing hotter now
  Since Andy crossed the Darling.

Oh, may the showers in torrents fall,
  And all the tanks run over;
And may the grass grow green and tall
  In pathways of the drover;

And may good angels send the rain
  On desert stretches sandy;
And when the summer comes again
  God grant 'twill bring us Andy.

WHEN YOUR PANTS BEGIN TO GO

Henry Lawson

When you wear a cloudy collar and a shirt that isn't white,
And you cannot sleep for thinking how you'll reach tomorrow night,
You may be a man of sorrow, and on speaking terms with Care,
But as yet you're unacquainted with the Demon of Despair;
For I rather think that nothing heaps the trouble on your mind
Like the knowledge that your trousers badly need a patch behind.

I have noticed when misfortune strikes the hero of the play
That his clothes are worn and tattered in a most unlikely way;
And the gods applaud and cheer him while he whines and loafs around,
But they never seem to notice that his pants are mostly sound;
Yet, of course, he cannot help it, for our mirth would mock his care,
If the ceiling of his trousers showed the patches of repair.

You are none the less a hero if you elevate your chin
When you feel the pavement wearing through the leather, sock, and skin;
You are rather more heroic than are ordinary folk
If you scorn to fish for pity under cover of a joke;
You will face the doubtful glances of the people that you know;
But — of course, you're bound to face them when your pants begin to go.

If, when flush, you took your pleasure — failed to make a god of Pelf —
Some will say that for your troubles you can only thank yourself;
Some will swear you'll die a beggar, but you only laugh at that
While your garments hang together and you wear a decent hat;
You may laugh at their predictions while your soles are wearing through —
But a man's an awful coward when his pants are going too!

Though the present and the future may be anything but bright,
It is best to tell the fellows that you're getting on all right.
And a man prefers to say it — 'tis a manly lie to tell,
For the folks may be persuaded that you're doing very well;
But it's hard to be a hero, and it's hard to wear a grin,
When your most important garment is in places very thin.

Get some sympathy and comfort from the chum who knows you best,
Then your sorrows won't run over in the presence of the rest;
There's a chum that you can go to when you feel inclined to whine,
He'll declare your coat is tidy, and he'll say: "Just look at mine!"
Though you may be patched all over he will say it doesn't show,
And he'll swear it can't be noticed when your pants begin to go.

Brother mine, and of misfortune! times are hard, but do not fret,
Keep your courage up and struggle, and we'll laugh at these things yet.
Though there is no corn in Egypt, surely Africa has some —
Keep your smile in working order for the better days to come!
We shall often laugh together at the hard times that we know,
And get measured by the tailor when our pants begin to go.

THE INTRO

C. J. Dennis

'Er name's Doreen . . . Well, spare me bloomin' days!
You could er knocked me down wiv 'arf a brick!
  Yes, me, that kids meself I know their ways,
  An' 'as a name for smoogin' in our click!
I just lines up an' tips the saucy wink.
But strike! The way she piled on dawg! Yer'd think
  A bloke was givin' back-chat to the Queen. . . .
    'Er name's Doreen.

I seen 'er in the markit first uv all,
Inspectin' brums at Steeny Isaac's stall.
  I backs me barrer in — the same ole way —
  An' sez, "Wot O! It's been a bonzer day.
'Ow is it fer a walk?" . . . Oh, 'oly wars!
The sorter *look* she gimme! Jest becors
  I tried to chat 'er, like you'd make a start
    Wiv *any* tart.

An' I kin take me oaf I was perlite,
An' never said no word that wasn't right,
  An' never tried to maul 'er, or to do
  A thing yeh might call crook. Ter tell yer true,
I didn't seem to 'ave the nerve — wiv 'er.
I felt as if I couldn't go that fur,
  An' start to sling off chiack like I used . . .
    Not intrajuiced!

Nex' time I sighted 'er in Little Bourke,
Where she was in a job, I found 'er lurk
  Was pastin' labels in a pickle joint,
  A game that — any'ow, that ain't the point.
Once more I tried ter chat 'er in the street,

But, bli'me! Did she turn me down a treat!
  The way she tossed 'er 'ead an' swished 'er skirt!
    Oh, it wus dirt!

A squarer tom, I swear, I never seen,
In all me natchril, than this 'ere Doreen.
  It wer'n't no guyver neither; fer I knoo
  That any other bloke 'ad Buckley's 'oo
Tried fer to pick 'er up. Yes, she was square.
She jist sailed by an' lef' me standin' there
  Like any mug. Thinks I, "I'm out er luck,"
    An' done a duck.

Well, I dunno. It's that way wiv a bloke.
If she'd ha' breasted up ter me an' spoke,
  I'd thort 'er jist a commin bit er fluff,
  An' then fergot about 'er, like enough.
It's jest like this. The tarts that's 'ard ter get
Make's you all 'ot to chase 'em, an' to let
  The cove called Cupid get an 'ammerlock;
    An' lose yer block.

I know a bloke 'oo knows a bloke 'oo toils
In that same pickle found-ery. ('E boild
  The cabbitch storks or somethink.) Anyway,
  I gives me pal the orfis fer to say
'E 'as a sister in the trade 'oo's been
Out uv a jorb, an' wants ter meet Doreen;
  Then we kin get an intro, if we've luck.
    'E sez, "Ribuck."

O' course we worked the oricle, you bet!
But, 'struth, I ain't recovered from it yet!
  'Twas on a Saturdee, in Collins Street,
  An' — quite by accident, o' course — we meet.

[Me pal 'e trots . . .

Me pal 'e trots 'er up an' does the toff —
'E allus wus a bloke fer showin' off.
"This 'ere's Doreen," 'e sez. "This 'ere's the Kid."
I dips me lid.

"This 'ere's Doreen," 'e sez. I sez "Good day."
An' bli'me, I 'ad nothin' more to say!
I couldn't speak a word, or meet 'er eye.
Clean done me block! I never been so shy,
Not since I was a tiny little cub,
An' run the rabbit to the corner pub —
Wot time the Summer days wus dry an' 'ot —
Fer me old pot.

Me! that 'as barracked tarts, an' torked an larft,
An' chucked orf at 'em like a phonergraft!
Gorstrooth! I seemed to lose me pow'r o' speech,
But 'er! Oh, strike me pink! She is a peach!
The sweetest in the barrer! Spare me days,
I can't describe that cliner's winnin' ways.
The way she torks! 'Er lips! 'Er eyes! 'Er hair! . . .
Oh, gimme air!

I dunno 'ow I done it in the end.
I reckerlect I arst ter be 'er friend;
An' tried ter play at 'andies in the park,
A thing she wouldn't sight. Aw, it's a nark!
I gotter swear when I think wot a mug
I must 'a' seemed to 'er. But still I 'ug
That promise that she give me fer the beach.
The bonzer peach!

Now, as the poit sez, the days drag by
On ledding feet. I wisht they'd do a guy.
I dunno 'ow I 'ad the nerve ter speak,
An' make that meet wiv 'er fer Sundee week!
But strike! It's funny wot a bloke'll do

When 'e's all out. . . . She's gorn, when I come-to.
  I'm yappin' to me cobber uv me mash. . . .
    I've done me dash!

'Er name's Doreen. . . . An' me — that thort I knoo
  The ways uv tarts, an' all that smoogin' game!
An' so I ort; fer ain't I known a few?
  Yet some'ow . . . I dunno. It ain't the same.
I can't tell *wot* it is; but, all I know,
I've dropped me bundle — an' I'm glad it's so.
  Fer when I come ter think uv wot I been. . . .
    'Er name's Doreen.

THE SHEARING-SHED

Henry Lawson

"The ladies are coming," the super says
  To the shearers sweltering there,
And "the ladies" means in the shearing-shed:
  "Don't cut 'em too bad. Don't swear."
The ghost of a pause in the shed's rough heart,
  And lower is bowed each head;
Then nothing is heard save a whispered word
  And the roar of the shearing-shed.

The tall, shy rouser has lost his wits;
  His limbs are all astray;
He leaves a fleece on the shearing-board
  And his broom in the shearer's way.
There's a curse in store for that jackeroo
  As down by the wall he slants —
But the ringer bends with his legs askew
  And wishes he'd "patched them pants".

They are girls from the city. Our hearts rebel
  As we squint at their dainty feet,
While they gush and say in a girly way
  That "the dear little lambs" are "sweet".
And Bill the Ringer, who'd scorn the use
  Of a childish word like damn,
Would give a pound that his tongue were loose
  As he tackles a lively lamb.

Swift thought of home in the coastal towns —
  Or rivers and waving grass —
And a weight on our hearts that we cannot define

[That comes as . . .

That comes as the ladies pass;
But the rouser ventures a nervous dig
With his thumb in the next man's back;
And Bogan says to his pen-mate: "Twig
The style of that last un, Jack."

Jack Moonlight gives her a careless glance —
Then catches his breath with pain;
His strong hand shakes, and the sunbeams dance
As he bends to his work again.
But he's well disguised in a bristling beard,
Bronzed skin, and his shearer's dress;
And whatever he knew or hoped or feared
Was hard for his mates to guess.

Jack Moonlight, wiping his broad, white brow,
Explains, with a doleful smile,
"A stitch in the side," and "I'm all right now" —
But he leans on the beam awhile,
And gazes out in the blazing noon
On the clearing, brown and bare. . . .
She had come and gone — like a breath of June
In December's heat and glare.

STRINGY-BARK AND GREEN-HIDE

Anon

I sing of a commodity, it's one that will not fail yer,
I mean that common oddity, the mainstay of Australia;
Gold it is a precious thing, for commerce it increases,
But stringy-bark and green-hide, can beat it all to pieces.

Chorus:
Stringy-bark and green-hide, they will never fail yer!
Stringy-bark and green-hide are the mainstay of Australia!

If you travel on the road, and chance to stick in Bargo,
To avoid a bad capsize, you must unload your cargo;
For to pull your dray about, I do not see the force on,
Take a bit of green-hide, and hook another horse on.

If you chance to take a dray, and break your leader's traces,
Get a bit of green-hide, to mend your broken places;
Green-hide is a useful thing, all that you require,
But stringy-bark's another thing when you want a fire.

If you want to build a hut, to keep out wind and weather,
Stringy-bark will make it snug, and keep it well together;
Green-hide if it's used by you, will make it all the stronger,
For if you tie it with green-hide, it's sure to last the longer.

New chums to this golden land, never dream of failure,
Whilst you've got such useful things as these in fair Australia.
For stringy-bark and green-hide will never, never fail yer,
Stringy-bark and green-hide are the mainstay of Australia.

WHO'S RIDING OLD HARLEQUIN NOW?

Harry ("The Breaker") Morant

They are mustering cattle on Brigalow Vale
Where the stock-horses whinny and stamp,
And where long Andy Ferguson, you may go bail,
Is yet boss on a cutting-out camp.
Half the duffers I met would not know a fat steer
From a blessed old Alderney cow;
Whilst they are mustering there I am wondering here —
Who is riding brown Harlequin now?

Are the pikers as wild and the scrubs just as dense
In the brigalow country as when
There was never a homestead and never a fence
Between Brigalow Vale and The Glen?
Do they yard the big micks 'neath the light of the moon?
Do the yard-wings re-echo the row
Of stockwhips and hoof-beats? And what sort of coon
Is there riding old Harlequin now?

There was buckjumping blood in the brown gelding's veins,
But, lean-headed, with iron-like pins,
Of Pyrrhus and Panic he'd plentiful strains,
All their virtues, and some of their sins.
'Twas pity, some said, that so shapely a colt
Fate should with such temper endow;
He would kick and would strike, he would buck and would bolt
Ah! who's riding brown Harlequin now?

A demon to handle! a devil to ride!
Small wonder the surcingle burst;
You'd have thought that he'd buck himself out of his hide
On the morning we saddled him first.
I can mind how he cow-kicked the spur on my boot,

And though that's long ago, still I vow
If they're wheeling a piker no new-chum galoot
Is a-riding old Harlequin now!

I remember the boss — how he chuckled and laughed
When they yarded the brown colt for me:
"He'll be steady enough when we finish the graft
And have cleaned up the scrubs of Glen Leigh!"
I am wondering today if the brown horse yet live,
For the fellow who broke him, I trow,
A long lease of soul-ease would willingly give
To be riding brown Harlequin now!

"Do you think you can hold him?" old Ferguson said —
He was mounted on Hornet, the grey;
I think Harlequin heard him — he shook his lean head,
And he needed no holding that day.
Not a prick from a spur, not a sting from a whip
As he raced among deadwood and bough
While I sat fairly quiet and just let him rip —
But who's riding old Harlequin now?

I could here 'em a-crashing the gidgee in front
As the Bryan colt streaked to the lead
Whilst the boss and the niggers were out of the hunt,
For their horses lacked Harlequin's speed;
The pikers were yarded and skies growing dim
When old Fergie was fain to allow:
"That colt's track through the scrub was a knocker" to him —
But who's riding brown Harlequin now?

From starlight to starlight — all day in between
The foam-flakes might fly from his bit,
But whatever the pace of the day's work had been
The brown gelding was eager and fit.

[On the packhorse's back . . .

On the packhorse's back they are fixing a load
Where the path climbs the hill's gloomy brow;
They are mustering bullocks to send on the road,
But — who's riding old Harlequin now?

WHITE BIRDS

Roland Robinson

White birds, frightened from silver grass,
whose blood-rose breasts and wings are thrown
like petals settling down the pass,
flower the ruined homestead's stone.

Rise from the fallen walls and scream,
crested, from the stark dead gum;
shatter the crystal of the morning's dream
where I, across your landscape, come.

Roofless, the broken stonework frames
red arid hills, a valley where
the ghost-gums writhe like whitened flames
and desert-oaks droop their dark hair.

And when in the crucible of the hills
the molten day has died, there stands,
under the blaze of stars that fills
its night, a house not made with hands.

WHERE THE PELICAN BUILDS

Mary Hannay Foott

The horses were ready, the rails were down,
But the riders lingered still —
One had a parting word to say,
And one had his pipe to fill.
Then they mounted, one with a granted prayer,
And one with a grief unguessed.
"We are going," they said as they rode away,
"Where the pelican builds her nest!"

They had told us of pastures wide and green,
To be sought past the sunset's glow;
Of rifts in the ranges by opal lit;
And gold 'neath the river's flow.
And thirst and hunger were banished words
When they spoke of that unknown West;
No drought they dreaded, no flood they feared,
Where the pelican builds her nest!

The creek at the ford was but fetlock deep
When we watched them crossing there;
The rains have replenished it thrice since then,
And thrice has the rock lain bare.
But the waters of Hope have flowed and fled,
And never from blue hill's breast
Come back — by the sun and the sands devoured —
Where the pelican builds her nest.

THE SICK STOCKRIDER

Adam Lindsay Gordon

Hold hard, Ned! Lift me down once more, and lay me in the shade.
Old man, you've had your work cut out to guide
Both horses, and to hold me in the saddle when I sway'd,
All through the hot, slow, sleepy, silent ride.

The dawn at "Moorabinda" was a mist rack dull and dense,
The sunrise was a sullen, sluggish lamp;
I was dozing in the gateway at Arbuthnot's bound'ry fence,
I was dreaming on the limestone cattle camp.

We crossed the creek at Carricksford, and sharply through the haze,
And suddenly, the sun shot flaming forth;
To the southward lay "Katawa", with the sandpeaks all ablaze,
And the flush'd fields of Glen Lomond lay to north.

Now westward winds the bridle path that leads to Lindisfarm,
And yonder looms the double-headed Bluff;
From the far side of the first hill, when the skies are clear and calm,
You can see Sylvester's woolshed fair enough.

Five miles we used to call it from our homestead to the place
Where the big tree spans the roadway like an arch;
'Twas here we ran the dingo down that gave us such a chase
Eight years ago — or was it nine? — last March.

'Twas merry in the glowing morn, among the gleaming grass,
To wander as we've wandered many a mile,
And blow the cool tobacco cloud, and watch the white wreaths pass,
Sitting loosely in the saddle all the while.

'Twas merry 'mid the blackwoods, when we spied the station roofs,
To wheel the wild scrub cattle at the yard,

With a running fire of stockwhips and a fiery run of hoofs;
Oh! the hardest day was never then too hard!

Aye! we had a glorious gallop after "Starlight" and his gang,
When they bolted from Sylvester's on the flat;
How the sun-dried reed-beds crackled, how the flint-strewn ranges rang
To the strokes of "Mountaineer" and "Acrobat"!

Hard behind them in the timber, harder still across the heath,
Close beside them through the tea-tree scrib we dashed;
And the golden-tinted fern leaves, how they rustled underneath!
And the honeysuckle osiers, how they crash'd!

We led the hunt throughout, Ned, on the chestnut and the grey,
And the troopers were three hundred yards behind,
While we emptied our six-shooters on the bushrangers at bay,
In the creek with stunted box-tree for a blind!

There you grappled with the leader, man to man and horse to horse,
And you roll'd together when the chestnut rear'd;
He blazed away and missed you in that shallow watercourse —
A narrow shave — his powder singed your beard!

In these hours when life is ebbing, how those days when life was young
Come back to us; how clearly I recall
Even the yarns Jack Hall invented, and the songs Jem Roper sung;
And where are now Jem Roper and Jack Hall?

Aye! nearly all our comrades of the old colonial school,
Our ancient boon companions, Ned, are gone:
Hard livers for the most part, somewhat reckless as a rule,
It seems that you and I are left alone.

There was Hughes, who got in trouble through that business with the cards,
It matters little what became of him;

[But a steer ripp'd up . . .

But a steer ripp'd up MacPherson in the Cooraminta yards,
And Sullivan was drown'd at Sink-or-swim.
And Mostyn — poor Frank Mostyn — died at last a fearful wreck,
In "the horrors", at the Upper Wandinong;
And Carisbrooke, the rider, at the Horsefall broke his neck —
Faith! the wonder was, he saved his neck so long!

Ah! those days and nights we squandered at the Logans' in the glen —
The Logans, man and wife, have long been dead.
Elsie's tallest girl seems taller than your little Elsie then;
And Ethel is a woman grown and wed.

I've had my share of pastime, and I've done my share of toil,
And life is short — the longest life a span;
I care not now to tarry for the corn or for the oil,
Or for the wine that maketh glad the heart of man.

For good undone and gifts misspent and resolutions vain,
'Tis somewhat late to trouble. This I know —
I should live the same life over, if I had to live again;
And the chances are I go where most men go.

The deep blue skies wax dusky, and the tall green trees grow dim,
The sward beneath me seems to heave and fall;
And sickly, smoky shadows through the sleepy sunlight swim,
And on the very sun's face weave their pall.

Let me slumber in the hollow where the wattle blossoms wave,
With never stone or rail to fence my bed;
Should the sturdy station children pull the bush flowers on my grave,
I may chance to hear them romping overhead.

I don't suppose I shall, though, for I feel like sleeping sound.
That sleep they say is doubtful. True; but yet
At least it makes no difference to the dead man underground
What the living men remember or forget.

Enigmas that perplex us in the world's unequal strife,
The future may ignore or may reveal.
YET SOME, AS WEAK AS WATER, NED! TO MAKE THE BEST OF LIFE,
HAVE BEEN, TO FACE THE WORST, AS TRUE AS STEEL.

ON THE NIGHT TRAIN

Henry Lawson

Have you seen the Bush by moonlight from the train go running by,
Here a patch of glassy water, there a glimpse of mystic sky?
Have you heard the still voice calling, yet so warm, and yet so cold:
"I'm the Mother-Bush that bore you! Come to me when you are old"?

Did you see the bush below you sweeping darkly to the range,
All unchanged and all unchanging, yet so very old and strange!
Did you hear the Bush a-calling, when your heart was young and bold:
"I'm the Mother-Bush that nursed you! Come to me when you are old"?

Through the long, vociferous cutting as the night train swiftly sped,
Did you hear the grey Bush calling from the pine-ridge overhead:
"You have seen the seas and cities; all seems done, and all seems told;
I'm the Mother-Bush that loves you! Come to me, now you are old"?

SOLITUDE

Henry Parkes

Where the mocking lyre-bird calls
To its mate among the falls
Of the mountain streams that play,
Each adown its tortuous way,
When the dewy-fingered even
Veils the narrow'd glimpse of Heaven:
Where the morning re-illumes
Gullies full of ferny plumes,
And a woof of radiance weaves
Through high-hanging vaults of leaves;
There, 'mid giant turpentines,
Groups of climbing, clustering vines,
Rocks that stand like sentinels,
Guarding Nature's citadels;
Lowly flowering shrubs that grace
With their beauty all the place —
There I love to wander lonely,
With my dog companion only;
There indulge unworldly moods
In the mountain solitudes;
Far from all the gilded strife
Of our boasted "social life",
Contemplating, spirit-free,
The majestic company
Grandly marching through the ages —
Heroes, martyrs, bards, and sages —
They who bravely suffered long,
By their struggles waxing strong,
For the freedom of the mind,
For the rights of humankind!
Oh, for some awakening cause,
Where we face eternal laws,

Where we dare not turn aside,
Where the souls of men are tried —
Something of the nobler strife
Which consumes the dross of life,
To unite to truer aim,
To exalt to loftier fame!
Leave behind the bats and balls,
Leave the racers in the stalls,
Leave the cards forever shuffled,
Leave the yacht on seas unruffled,
Leave the haunts of pampered ease,
Leave your dull festivities! —
Better far the savage glen,
Fitter school for earnest men!

DROUGHT

Will H. Ogilvie

My road is fenced with the bleached, white bones,
  And strewn with the blind, white sand,
Beside me a suffering, dumb world moans
  On the breast of a lonely land.

On the rim of the world the lightnings play,
  The heat-waves quiver and dance,
And the breath of the wind is a sword to slay,
  And the sunbeams each a lance.

I have withered the grass where my hot hoofs tread,
  I have whitened the sapless trees,

[I have driven . . .

I have driven the faint-heart rains ahead
  To hide in their soft green seas.

I have bound the plains with an iron band,
  I have stricken the slow streams dumb!
To the charge of my vanguards who shall stand?
  Who slay when my cohorts come?

The dust-storms follow and wrap me round,
  The hot winds ride as a guard;
Before me the fret of the swamps is bound
  And the way of the wild-fowl barred.

I drop the whips on the loose-flanked steers;
  I burn their necks with the bow;
And the greenhide rips and the iron sears
  Where the staggering lean beasts go.

I lure the swagman out of the road
  To the gleam of a phantom lake;
I have laid him down, I have taken his load,
  And he sleeps till the dead men wake.

My hurrying hoofs in the night go by,
  And the great flocks bleat their fear,
And follow the curve of the creeks burnt dry
  And the plains scorched brown and sere.

The worn men start from their sleepless rest
  With faces haggard and drawn;
They cursed the red sun into the west
  And they curse him out of the dawn.

They have carried their outposts far, far out,
  But — blade of my sword for a sign!
I am the Master, the dread King Drought,
  And the great West Land is mine!

SPRING ON THE PLAINS

Dorothea Mackellar

Spring has come to the plains,
And, following close behind,
Green of the welcome rains
And spice of the first warm wind.
Beating of wings on high,
For, overhead in the blue,
Southward the brolgas fly,
The cranes and pelicans, too,
Ibis and proud black swan —
And quivering cries float clear,
After the birds are gone,
Still lingering in the ear.

Everywhere we pass
The horses tread soft and deep;
Clover and young green grass —
Hark to the grazing sheep
Cropping steady and slow —
A peaceful, satisfied sound:
Thick on the paths we go,
Gold flowers are starring the ground.
Spring, and the world's astir,
And everything gives praise,
Singing the strength of her
These lovely lengthening days.

BILL BROWN

Edward S. Sorenson

I met Bill Brown on the Prospect Track
Astride of a camel cow;
An' I said, "I heard you had got the sack,
An' where are you makin' now?"

"Well, mate," said William, "I thought it out,
An' I sez to myself, sez I:
There's not much hope for the rouseabout,
As the rousy can testify.

"So I'll drink the honey of Freedom's Cup,
An' do as it pleases Brown;
I'll roll me swag when the sun gets up,
An' I'll camp when the sun goes down.

"I'm makin' out where the diggers go,
Where the reefs run deep an' wide;
I'll wet my whistle at Tally-ho,
An' I'll yard me a Western bride.

"She'll make me rugs with the skins I get
When I'm off o' the veins of gold;
She'll strip an' thatch when the days are wet,
An' she'll stoke when the nights are cold.

"With only a fire in the trackless zone,
She'll cook like a chef, bet you;
Whatever she needs she will find alone
For her salmagundi too.

"If the tracks are barren this moke I've got
Will do with a mulga-tree,

An' the hobble-chains an' the old quart-pot
Still jingle a tune to me."

He filled his pipe ere he said, "So long!"
An' he rode where the sun grows red;
Where the bold are lured with a golden song
At times to a dead man's bed.

Though many ask, 'tis a nut to crack,
Where old Bill Brown is now;
He was heard of last on the Prospect Track
Astride of a camel cow.

AROUND THE BOREE LOG

P. J. Hartigan
("John O'Brien")

Oh, stick me in the old caboose this night of wind and rain,
And let the doves of fancy loose to bill and coo again.
I want to feel the pulse of love that warmed the blood like wine;
I want to see the smile above this kind old land of mine.

So come you by your parted ways that wind the wide world through,
And make a ring around the blaze the way we used to do;
The "fountain" on the sooted crane will sing the old, old song
Of common joys in homely vein forgotten, ah, too long.

The years have turned the rusty key, and time is on the jog,
Yet spend another night with me around the boree log.

[Now someone driving . . .

Now someone driving through the rain will happen in, I bet;
So fill the fountain up again, and leave the table set.
For this was ours with pride to say — and all the world defy —
No stranger ever turned away, no neighbour passed us by.

Bedad, he'll have to stay the night; the rain is going to pour —
So make the rattling windows tight, and close the kitchen door,
And bring the old lopsided chair, the tattered cushion, too —
We'll make the stranger happy there, the way we used to do.

The years have turned the rusted key, and time is on the jog,
Yet spend another night with me around the boree log.

He'll fill his pipe, and good and well, and all aglow within
We'll hear the news he has to tell, the yarns he has to spin;
Yarns — yes, and super-yarns, forsooth, to set the eyes agog,
And freeze the blood of trusting youth around the boree log.

Then stir it up and make it burn; the poker's next to you;
Come, let us poke it all in turn, the way we used to do.
There's many a memory bright and fair will tingle at a name —
But leave unstirred the embers there we cannot fan to flame.

For years have turned the rusted key, and time is on the jog;
Still, spend this fleeting night with me around the boree log.

THE FIRE AT ROSS'S FARM

Henry Lawson

The squatter saw his pastures wide
  Decrease, as one by one
The farmers moving to the west
  Selected on his run;
Selectors took the water up
  And all the black-soil round;
The best grass-land the squatter had
  Was spoilt by Ross's ground.

Now many schemes to shift old Ross
  Had racked the squatter's brains,
But Sandy had the stubborn blood
  Of Scotland in his veins;
He held the land and fenced it in,
  He cleared and ploughed the soil,
And year by year a richer crop
  Repaid him for his toil.

Between the homes for many years
  The devil left his tracks:
The squatter 'pounded Ross's stock,
  And Sandy 'pounded Black's.
A well upon the lower run
  Was filled with earth and logs,
And Black laid baits about the farm
  To poison Ross's dogs.

It was, indeed, a deadly feud
  Of class and creed and race.
So Fate supplied a Romeo

[And a Juliet . . .

And a Juliet in the case;
and more than once across the flats,
Beneath the Southern Cross,
Young Robert Black was seen to ride
With pretty Jenny Ross.

One Christmas time, when months of drought
Had parched the western creeks,
The bush-fires started in the north
And travelled south for weeks.
At night along the river-side
The scene was grand and strange —
The hill-fires looked like lighted streets
Of cities in the range.

The cattle-tracks between the trees
Were like long dusky aisles,
And on a sudden breeze the fire
Would sweep along for miles;
Like sounds of distant musketry
It crackled through the brakes,
And o'er the flat of silver grass
It hissed like angry snakes.

It leapt across the flowing streams
And raced the pastures through;
It climbed the trees, and lit the boughs,
And fierce and fiercer grew.
The bees fell stifled in the smoke
Or perished in their hives,
And with the stock the kangaroos
Went flying for their lives.

The sun had set on Christmas Eve,
When through the scrub-lands wide
Young Robert Black came riding home
As only natives ride.

He galloped to the homestead door
  And gave the first alarm:
"The fire is past the granite spur,
  And close to Ross's farm.

"Now, father, send the men at once,
  They won't be wanted here;
Poor Ross's wheat is all he has
  To pull him through the year."
"Then let it burn," the squatter said;
  "I'd like to see it done —
I'd bless the fire if it would clear
  Selectors from the run.

"Go if you will," the squatter said,
  "You shall not take the men —
Go out and join your precious friends,
  But don't come here again."
"I won't come back," young Robert cried,
  And reckless in his ire,
He sharply turned the horse's head
  And galloped towards the fire.

And there for three long weary hours,
  Half-blind with smoke and heat,
Old Ross and Robert fought the flames
  That neared the ripened wheat.
The farmer's hand was nerved by fear
  Of danger and of loss;
And Robert fought the stubborn foe
  For love of Jenny Ross.

But serpent-like the curves and lines
Slipped past them, and between
Until they reached the boundary where

[The old coach-road . . .

The old coach-road had been.
"The track is now our only hope.
There we must stand," cried Ross.
'For naught on earth can stop the fire
If once it gets across."

Then came a cruel gust of wind,
And, with a fiendish rush,
The flames leapt o'er the narrow path
And lit the fence of brush.
"The crop must burn!" the farmer cried.
"We cannot save it now."
And down upon the blackened ground
He dashed his ragged bough.

But wildly, in a rush of hope,
His heart began to beat,
For o'er the crackling fire he heard
The sound of horses' feet.
"Here's help at last," young Robert cried,
And even as he spoke
The squatter with a dozen men
Came racing through the smoke.

Down on the ground the stockmen jumped
And bared each brawny arm;
They tore green branches from the trees
And fought for Ross's farm;
And when before the gallant band
The beaten flames gave way.
Two grimy hands in friendship joined —
And it was Christmas Day.

COUNTRY PRESS

Rosemary Dobson

Under the dusty print of hobnailed boot,
Strewn on the floor the papers still assert
In ornamental gothic, swash italics
And bands of printer's flowers (traditional)
Mixed in a riot of typographic fancy,
This is the *Western Star*, the Farmer's Guide,
The Voice of Progress for the Nyngle District.
Page-proofs of double-spread with running headlines
Paper the walls, and sets of cigarette cards
Where pouter-bosomed showgirls still display
The charms that dazzled in the nineteen hundreds.
Through gaping slats
Latticed with sun the ivy tendrils fall
Twining the disused platen thrust away
Under a pall of dust in nineteen-twenty.
Draw up a chair, sit down. Just shift the galleys.
You say you have a notice? There's no one dies
But what we know about it. Births, deaths and marriages,
Council reports, wool prices, river-heights,
The itinerant poem and the classified ads —
They all come homewards to the *Western Star*.
Joe's our type-setter. Meet Joe Burrell. Joe's
A promising lad — and Joe, near forty-seven,
Peers from a tennis-shade and, smiling vaguely,
Completes the headlines for the Baptist Social.
The dance, the smoke-oh, and the children's picnic
Down by the river-flats beneath the willows —
They all come homewards and Joe sets them all,
Between the morning and the mid-day schooner.
Oh, *Western Star* that bringest all to fold,

[The yarding sales . . .

The yarding sales, the champion shorthorn bull,
And William's pain-relieving liniment,
When I shall die
Set me up close against my fellow-men,
Cheer that cold column headed "Deaths" with flowers,
Or mix me up with Births and Marriages;
Surround the tragic statement of my death
With euchre-drives and good-times-had-by-all
That, with these warm concomitants of life
Jostled and cheered, in lower-case italics
I shall go homewards in the *Western Star.*

PLACE NAMES

Douglas Stewart

Ethadinna, Mira Mitta,
Mulka, Mungerannie —
Dark shadows blown
With the dust away,
Far from our day
Far out of time,
Fill the land with water.
Where the blue sky flames
On the bare red stone,
Dulkaninna, Koperamanna,
Ooroowilanie, Kilalpaninna —
Only the names
In the land remain
Like a dark well
Like the chime of a bell.

THE DROVERS

Roland Robinson

Over the plains of the whitening grass
and the stunted mulga the drovers pass,
and in the red dust cloud, each side
of the cattle, the native stockmen ride.

And day after day lays bare the same
endless plains as the way they came,
and ever the cloven ranges lie
at the end of the land and the opal sky.

With creak of pack and saddle leather,
and chink of chain and bit together,
with moan of the herd, with hobble and bell
they come to the tanks at the tea-tree well.

And through corroding blood-red hills,
by sanded rivers the Gulf-rain fills,
far, where the morning star has shone
and paled above, their tracks are gone.

THE SUNDOWNER

John Shaw Neilson

I know not when this tiresome man
With his shrewd, sable billy-can
And his unwashed Democracy
His boomed-up Pilgrimage began.

Sometimes he wandered far outback
On a precarious Tucker Track;
Sometimes he lacked Necessities
No gentleman would like to lack.

Tall was the grass, I understand,
When the old Squatter ruled the land.
Why were the Conquerors kind to him?
Ah, the Wax Matches in his hand!

Where bullockies with oaths intense
Made of the dragged-up trees a fence,
Gambling with scorpions he rolled
His Swag, conspicuous, immense.

In the full splendour of his power
Rarely he touched one mile an hour,
Dawdling at sunset, History says,
For the Pint Pannikin of flour.

Seldom he worked; he was, I fear,
Unreasonably slow and dear;
Little he earned, and that he spent
Deliberately drinking Beer.

[Cheerful, sorefooted child . . .

Cheerful, sorefooted child of chance,
Swiftly we knew him at a glance;
Boastful and self-compassionate,
Australia's Interstate Romance.

Shall he not live in Robust Rhyme,
Soliloquies and Odes Sublime?
Strictly between ourselves, he was
A rare old Humbug all the time.

In many a Book of Bushland dim
Mopokes shall give him greeting grim;
The old swans pottering in the reeds
Shall pass the time of day to him.

On many a page our Friend shall take
Small sticks his evening fire to make;
Shedding his waistcoat, he shall mix
On its smooth back his Johnny-Cake.

'Mid the dry leaves and silvery bark
Often at nightfall will he park
Close to a homeless creek, and hear
The Bunyip paddling in the dark.

HIGH PLACES

Dorothea Mackellar

My heart turns to the mountains
That I so long have missed,
The blue hills on the sky-line,
Bird-haunted, sunshine-kissed;
For in my soul I see them,
The gullies golden-green
Where from the hop-vine tangle
The bellbird chimes unseen.

And higher yet and higher
I want to climb, until
The trees give place to bushes
Wind-shorn and struggling still
For foothold on the corries
Steep-sloping to the sky,
I want to reach the summit
And watch the clouds race by

The clouds that go so quickly
The whole hill seems to lean
I want to breathe in deeply
The cool air, thin and keen.
My heart turns to high places
All men have long adored —
The proud and lonely mountains,
The Altars of the Lord.

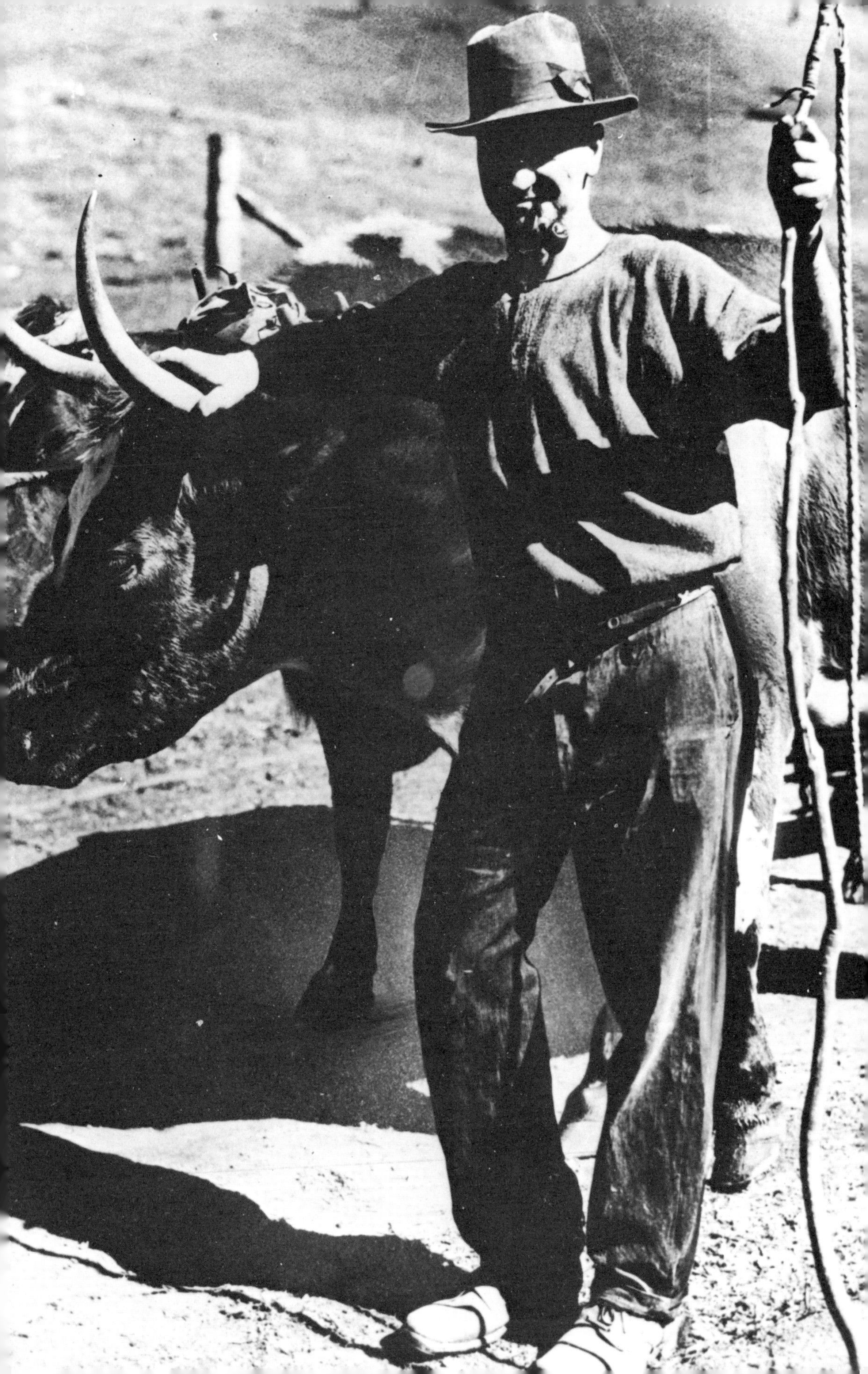

BULLOCKY

Judith Wright

Beside his heavy-shouldered team,
thirsty with drought and chilled with rain,
he weathered all the striding years
till they ran widdershins in his brain:

Till the long solitary tracks
etched deeper with each lurching load
were populous before his eyes,
and fiends and angels used his road.

All the straining journey grew
a mad apocalyptic dream,
and he old Moses, and the slaves
his suffering and stubborn team.

Then is his evening camp beneath
the half-light pillars of the trees
he filled the steepled cone of night
with shouted prayers and prophecies.

While past the campfire's crimson ring
the star-struck darkness cupped him round,
and centuries of cattle-bells
rang with their sweet uneasy sound.

Grass is across the wagon-tracks,
and plough strikes bone across the grass,
and vineyards cover all the slopes
where the dead teams were used to pass.

[O vine, grow close . . .

O vine, grow close upon that bone
and hold it with your rooted hand.
The prophet Moses feeds the grape,
and fruitful is the Promised Land.

WALTZING MATILDA

A. B. ("Banjo") Paterson

Once a jolly swagman camped by a billabong,
  Under the shade of a coolibah tree,
And he sang as he watched and waited till his billy boiled,
  "Who'll come a-waltzing Matilda with me?
    Waltzing Matilda,
    Waltzing Matilda,
  Who'll come a-waltzing Matilda with me?"
And he sang as he watched and waited till his billy boiled,
  "Who'll come a-waltzing Matilda with me?"

Down came a jumbuck to drink at the billabong:
  Up jumped the swagman and grabbed him with glee.
And he sang as he shoved that jumbuck in his tucker-bag,
  "You'll come a-waltzing Matilda with me.
    Waltzing Matilda,
    Waltzing Matilda,
  You'll come a-waltzing Matilda with me."
And he sang as he shoved that jumbuck in his tucker-bag,
  "You'll come a-waltzing Matilda with me."

Up rode a squatter, mounted on his thoroughbred;
  Down came the troopers, one, two, three:
"Whose' that jolly jumbuck you've got in your tucker-bag?
  You'll come a-waltzing Matilda with me!
    Waltzing Matilda,
    Waltzing Matilda,
  You'll come a-waltzing Matilda with me!
Whose' that jolly jumbuck you've got in your tucker-bag?
  You'll come a-waltzing Matilda with me!"

Up jumped the swagman and sprang into the billabong;
  "You'll never catch me alive!" said he;
And his ghost may be heard as you pass by that billabong,
  "You'll come a-waltzing Matilda with me!
    Waltzing Matilda,
    Waltzing Matilda,
  You'll come a-waltzing Matilda with me!"
And his ghost may be heard as you pass by that billabong,
  "You'll come a-waltzing Matilda with me!"

INDEPENDENCE

Nancy Cato

How the red road stretched before us, mile on mile
Narrowing into the distance, straight as though ruled
On yellow paper, away to the lilac hills
Low on the horizon. Above them the storm-clouds piled
In a sky blue as though bruised, yet all ahead
Was glowing in an unearthly wash of light,
Dry roly-poly and saltbush lit to beauty,
The sky a menace, but the wide plains bright.

And there in that lonely place an ancient swagman,
Traveller, bagman, sundowner, what you will —
His rolled-up blankets slung aslant his shoulders,
Billy dangling, his back to the line of hills
And the coming storm; as mysterious in that place
(With his hat set straight and his grey beard blowing)
As a small ship glimpsed a moment far from land.
Where did he come from, where could he be going?

I shall never know, for we had to race the rain
That turns the blacksoil plains to a gluey mud
Bogging to the axles. Only a wave of the hand,
But still the imagination glows, the blood
Stirs at the memory of that symbolic stranger
Glimpsed in a moment of vision and swiftly gone:
Man and his independent spirit, alone
On the vast plains, with night and rain coming on.

THE WOMEN OF THE WEST

George Essex Evans

They left the vine-wreathed cottage and the mansion on the hill,
The houses in the busy streets where life is never still,
The pleasures of the city, and the friends they cherished best:
For love they faced the wilderness — the Women of the West.

The roar, and rush, and fever of the city died away,
And the old-time joys and faces — they were gone for many a day;
In their place the lurching coach-wheel, or the creaking bullock chains,
O'er the everlasting sameness of the never-ending plains.

In the slab-built, zinc-roofed homestead of some lately-taken run,
In the tent beside the bankment of a railway just begun,
In the huts on new selections, in the camps of man's unrest,
On the frontiers of the Nation, live the women of the West.

The red sun robs their beauty, and, in weariness and pain,
The slow years steal the nameless grace that never comes again;
And there are hours men cannot soothe, and words men cannot say —
The nearest woman's face may be a hundred miles away.

The wide Bush holds the secrets of their longings and desires,
When the white stars in reverence light their holy altar-fires,
And silence, like the touch of god, sinks deep into the breast —
Perchance He hears and understands the Women of the West.

For them no trumpet sounds the call, no poet plies his arts —
They only hear the beating of their gallant, loving hearts,
But they have sung with silent lives the song all songs above —
The holiness of sacrifice, the dignity of love.

[Well have we held . . .

Well have we held our father's creed. No call has passed us by.
We faced and fought the wilderness, we sent our sons to die.
And we have hearts to do and dare, and yet, o'er all the rest,
The hearts that made the Nation were the Women of the West.

THE LIGHTS OF COBB AND CO.

Henry Lawson

Firelighted; on the table a meal for sleepy men;
A lantern in the stable; a jingle now and then;
The mail-coach looming darkly by light of moon and star;
The growl of sleepy voices; a candle in the bar;
A stumble in the passage of folk with wits abroad;
A swear-word from a bedroom — the shout of "All aboard!"
"Tchk tchk! Git-up!" "Hold fast, there!" and down the range we go;
Five hundred miles of scattered camps will watch for Cobb and Co.

Old coaching towns already decaying for their sins;
Uncounted "Half-Way Houses", and scores of "Ten-Mile Inns";
The riders from the stations by lonely granite peaks;
The black-boy for the shepherds on sheep and cattle creeks;
The roaring camps of Gulgong, and many a "Digger's Rest";
The diggers on the Lachlan; the huts of Farthest West;
Some twenty thousand exiles who sailed for weal or woe —
The bravest hearts of twenty lands will wait for Cobb and Co.

The morning star has vanished, the frost and fog are gone,
In one of those grand mornings which but on mountains dawn;
A flask of friendly whisky — each other's hopes we share —
And throw our top-coats open to drink the mountain air.
The roads are rare to travel, and life seems all complete;
The grind of wheels on gravel, the trot of horses' feet,
The trot, trot, trot and canter, as down the spur we go —
The green sweeps to horizons blue that call for Cobb and Co.

We take a bright girl actress through western dusts and damps,
To bear the home-world message, and sing for sinful camps,
To stir our hearts and break them, wild hearts that hope and ache —
(Ah! when she thinks again of these her own must nearly break!)
Five miles this side the gold-field, a loud, triumphant shout:
Five hundred cheering diggers have snatched the horses out:
With "Auld Lang Syne" in chorus, through roaring camps they go
That cheer for her, and cheer for Home, and cheer for Cobb and Co.

Three lamps above the ridges and gorges dark and deep,
A flash on sandstone cuttings where sheer the sidlings sweep,
A flash on shrouded waggons, on water ghastly white;
Weird bush and scattered remnants of "rushes in the night";
Across the swollen river a flash beyond the ford:
Ride hard to warn the driver! He's drunk or mad, good Lord!
But on the bank to westward a broad and cheerful glow —
New camps extend across the plains new routes for Cobb and Co.

THE MEN WHO MADE AUSTRALIA

(Written on the Occasion of the Royal Visit to Australia, 1901)

Henry Lawson

There'll be royal times in Sydney for the Cuff and Collar Push,
  There'll be lots of dreary drivel and clap-trap
From the men who own Australia, but who never knew the bush,
  And who could not point their runs out on the map.
Ho, the daily Press will grovel as it never did before,
  There'll be many flags of welcome in the air,
And the Civil Service poet, he shall write odes by the score —
  But the men who made the land will not be there.

You shall meet the awful Lady of the latest Birthday Knight —
  (She is trying to be English, don't-cher-know?)
You shall hear the empty mouthing of the champion blatherskite,
  You shall hear the boss of local drapers blow.
There's "majahs" from the counter, tailors' dummies from the fleet,
  And to represent Australia here today,
There's the toady with his card-case and his cab in Downing Street;
  But the men who made Australia — where are they?

Call across the blazing sand wastes of the Never-Never Land!
  There are some who will not answer yet awhile,
Some whose bones rot in the mulga or lie bleaching on the sand,
  Died of thirst to win the land another mile.
Thrown from horses, ripped by cattle, lost on deserts: and the weak,
  Mad through loneliness or drink (no matter which),
Drowned in floods or dead of fever by the sluggish slimy creek —
  These are men who died to make the Wool-Kings rich.

There are carriages in waiting for the swells from over-sea,
  There are banquets in the latest London style,

[While the men who made . . .

While the men who made Australia live on damper, junk and tea —
  But the quiet voices whisper, "Wait a while!"
For the sons of all Australia, they were born to conquer fate —
  And, where charity and friendship are sincere,
Where a sinner is a brother and a stranger is a mate,
  There the future of a nation's written clear.

Aye, the cities claim the triumphs of a land they do not know,
  But all empty is the day they celebrate!
For the men who made Australia federated long ago,
  And the men to rule Australia — they can wait.
Though the bed may be the rough bunk or the gum leaves or the sand,
  And the roof for half the year may be the sky — .
There are men among the Bushmen who were born to save the land!
  And they'll take their places sternly by-and-by.

MULGA BILL'S BICYCLE

A. B. ("Banjo") Paterson

'Twas Mulga Bill, from Eaglehawk, that caught the cycling craze;
He turned away the good old horse that served him many days;
He dressed himself in cycling clothes, resplendent to be seen;
He hurried off to town and bought a shining new maching;
And as he wheeled it through the door, with air of lordly pride,
The grinning shop assistant said, "Excuse me, can you ride?"

"See, here, young man," said Mulga Bill, "from Walgett to the sea,
From Conroy's Gap to Castlereagh, there's none can ride like me.
I'm good all round at everything, as everybody knows,
Although I'm not the one to talk — I *hate* a man that blows.
But riding is my special gift, my chiefest, sole delight;

Just ask a wild duck can it swim, a wild cat can it fight.
There's nothing clothed in hair or hide, or built of flesh or steel,
There's nothing walks or jumps or runs, on axle, hoof, or wheel,
But what I'll sit, while hide will hold and girths and straps are tight:
I'll ride this here two-wheeled concern right straight away at sight."

'Twas Mulga Bill, from Eaglehawk, that sought his own abode,
That perched above the Dead Man's Creek, beside the mountain road.
He turned the cycle down the hill and mounted for the fray,
But ere he'd gone a dozen yards it bolted clean away.
It left the track, and through the trees, just like a silver streak,
It whistled down the awful slope, towards the Dead Man's Creek.

It shaved a stump by half an inch, it dodged a big white-box:
The very wallaroos in fright went scrambling up the rocks,
The wombats hiding in their caves dug deeper underground,
As Mulga Bill, as white as chalk, sat tight to every bound.
It struck a stone and gave a spring that cleared a fallen tree,
It raced beside a precipice as close as close could be;
And then as Mulga Bill let out one last despairing shriek
It made a leap of twenty feet into the Dead Man's Creek.

'Twas Mulga Bill, from Eaglehawk, that slowly swam ashore:
He said, "I've had some narrer shaves and lively rides before;
I've rode a wild bull round a yard to win a five pound bet,
But this was the most awful ride that I've encountered yet.
I'll give that two-wheeled outlaw best; it's shaken all me nerve
To feel it whistle through the air and plunge and buck and swerve.
It's safe at rest in Dead Man's Creek, we'll leave it lying still;
A horse's back is good enough henceforth for Mulga Bill."

FROM THE WRECK

Adam Lindsay Gordon

"Turn out, boys" — "What's up with our super, tonight?
  The man's mad — Two hours to daybreak I'd swear —
Stark mad — why, there isn't a glimmer of light."
  "Take Bolingbroke, Alec, give Jack the young mare;
Look sharp. A large vessel lies jamm'd on the reef,
  And many on board still, and some wash'd on shore.
Ride straight with the news — they may send some relief
  From the township; and we — we can do little more.
You, Alec, you know the near cuts; you can cross
  The Sugarloaf ford with a scramble, I think;
Don't spare the blood filly, nor yet the black horse;
  Should the wind rise, God help them! the ship will soon sink.
Old Peter's away down the paddock, to drive
  The nags to the stockyard as fast as he can —
A life and death matter; so, lads, look alive."
  Half-dress'd, in the dark, to the stockyard we ran.

There was bridling with hurry, and saddling with haste,
  Confusion and cursing for lack of a moon;
"Be quick with those buckles; we've no time to waste";
  "Mind the mare, she can use her hind legs to some tune,"
"Make sure of the crossing-place; strike the old track,
  They've fenced off the new one; look out for the holes
On the wombat hills." "Down with the slip rails; stand back."
  "And ride, boys, the pair of you, ride for your souls."

In the low branches heavily laden with dew,
  In the long grasses spoiling with deadwood that day,
Where the blackwood, the box, and the bastard oak grew,
  Between the tall gum-trees we galloped away —
We crashed through a brush fence, we splashed through a swamp —
  We steered for the north near The Eaglehawk's Nest —

We bore to the left, just beyond The Red Camp,
  And round the black tea-tree belt wheel'd to the west —
We cross'd a low range sickly scented with musk
  From wattle-tree blossom — we skirted a marsh —
Then the dawn faintly dappled with orange the dusk,
  And peal'd overhead the jay's laughter note harsh,
And shot the first sunstreak behind us, and soon
  The dim dewy uplands were dreamy with light;
and full on our left flash'd The Reedy Lagoon,
  And sharply The Sugarloaf rear'd on our right.

A smother'd curse broke through the bushman's brown beard,
  He turn'd in the saddle, his brick-coloured cheek
Flash'd feebly with sundawn, said, "Just what I fear'd;
  Last fortnight's late rainfall has flooded the creek."

Black Bolingbroke snorted, and stood on the brink
  One instant, then deep in the dark sluggish swirl
Plunged headlong, I saw the horse suddenly sink,
  Till round the man's armpits the waves seem'd to curl.
We follow'd, — one cold shock, and deeper we sank
  Than they did, and twice tried the landing in vain;
The third struggle won it; straight up the steep bank
  We stagger'd, then out on the skirts of the plain.

The stockrider, Alec, at starting had got
  The lead, and had kept it throughout; 'twas his boast
That through thickest of scrub he could steer like a shot,
  And the black horse was counted the best on the coast.
The mare had been awkward enough in the dark,
  She was eager and headstrong, and barely half broke;
She had had me too close to a big stringy-bark,
  And had made a near thing of a crooked sheoak.

[But now on the open . . .

But now on the open, lit up by the morn,
  She flung the white foam-flakes from nostril to neck,
And chased him — I hatless, with shirt sleeves all torn
  (For he may ride ragged who rides from a wreck) —
And faster and faster across the wide heath
  We rode till we raced. Then I gave her her head,
and she — stretching out with the bit in her teeth —
  She caught him, outpaced him, and passed him, and led.

We neared the new fence; we were wide of the track;
  I look'd right and left — she had never been tried
At a stiff leap. 'Twas little he cared on the black.
  "You're more than a mile from the gateway," he cried.
I hung to her head, touched her flank with the spurs
  (In the red streak of rail not the ghost of a gap);
She shortened her long stroke, she pricked her sharp ears,
  She flung it behind her with hardly a rap —
I saw the post quiver where Bolingbroke struck,
  And guessed that the pace we had come the last mile
Had blown him a bit (he could jump like a buck).
  We galloped more steadily then for a while.

The heath was soon pass'd, in the dim distance lay
  The mountain. The sun was just clearing the tips
Of the ranges to eastward. The mare — could she stay?
  She was bred very nearly as clean as Eclipse;
She led, and as oft as he came to her side,
  She took the bit free and untiring as yet;
Her neck was arched double, her nostrils were wide,
  And the tips of her tapering ears nearly met —
"You're lighter than I am," said Alec at last;
  "The horse is dead beat and the mare isn't blown,
She must be a good one — ride on and ride fast,
  You know your way now." So I rode on alone.

Still galloping forward we pass'd the two flocks
  At M'Intyre's hut and M'Allister's hill —
She was galloping strong at the Warrigal Rocks —
  On the Wallaby Range she was galloping still —
And over the wasteland and under the wood,
  By down and by dale, and by fell and by flat,
She gallop'd. And here in the stirrups I stood
  To ease her, and there in the saddle I sat
To steer her. We suddenly struck the red loam
  Of the track near the troughs — then she reeled on the rise —
From her crest to her croup covered over with foam,
  And blood-red her nostrils and bloodshot her eyes,
A dip in the dell where the wattle fire bloomed
  A bend round a bank that had shut out the view —
Large framed in the mild light the mountain had loomed,
  With a tall, purple peak bursting out from the blue.

I pull'd her together, I press'd her, and she
  Shot down the decline to the Company's yard,
And on by the paddocks, yet under my knee
  I could feel her heart thumping the saddle-flaps hard.
Yet a mile and another, and now we were near
  The goal, and the fields and the farms flitted past;
And 'twixt the two fences I turned with a cheer,
  For a green, grass-fed mare 'twas a far thing and fast;
And labourers, roused by her galloping hoofs,
  Saw bare-headed rider and foam-sheeted steed;
And shone the white walls and the slate-coloured roofs
  Of the townships. I steadied her then — I had need —
Where stood the old chapel (where stands the new church —
  Since chapels to churches have changed in that town).
A short, sidelong stagger, a long, forward lurch,
  A slight choking sob, and the mare had gone down.
I slipp'd off the bridle, I slackened the girth,
  I ran on and left her and told them my news;
I saw her soon afterwards. What was she worth?
  How much for her hide? She had never worn shoes.

THE GEEBUNG POLO CLUB

A. B. ("Banjo") Paterson

It was somewhere up the country, in a land of rock and scrub,
That they formed an institution called the Geebung Polo Club.
They were long and wiry natives from the rugged mountain side,
And the horse was never saddled that the Geebungs couldn't ride;
But their style of playing polo was irregular and rash —
They had mighty little science, but a mighty lot of dash:
And they played on mountain ponies that were muscular and strong,
Though their coats were quite unpolished, and their manes and tails were long.
And they used to train those ponies wheeling cattle in the scrub;
They were demons, were the members of the Geebung Polo Club.

It was somewhere down the country, in a city's smoke and steam,
That a polo club existed, called "The Cuff and Collar Team".
As a social institution 'twas a marvellous success,
For the members were distinguished by exclusiveness and dress.
They had natty little ponies that were nice, and smooth, and sleek,
For their cultivated owners only rode 'em once a week.
So they started up the country in pursuit of sport and fame.
For they meant to show the Geebungs how they ought to play the game;
And they took their valets with them — just to give their boots a rub
Ere they started operations on the Geebung Polo Club.

Now my readers can imagine how the contest ebbed and flowed,
When the Geebung boys got going it was time to clear the road;
And the game was so terrific that ere half the time was gone
A spectator's leg was broken — just from merely looking on.
For they waddied one another till the plain was strewn with dead.
While the score was kept so even that they neither got ahead.
And the Cuff and Collar Captain, when he tumbled off to die
Was the last surviving player — so the game was called a tie.
Then the Captain of the Geebungs raised him slowly from the ground,
Though his wounds were mostly mortal, yet he fiercely gazed around;

There was no one to oppose him — all the rest were in a trance.
So he scrambled on his pony for his last expiring chance.
For he meant to make an effort to get the victory to his side;
So he struck at goal — and missed it — then he tumbled off and died.

By the old Campaspe River, where the breezes shake the grass,
There's a row of little gravestones that the stockmen never pass,
For they bear a rude inscription saying, "Stranger, drop a tear,
For the Cuff and Collar players and the Geebung boys lie here."
And on misty moonlit evenings, while the dingoes howl around,
You can see their shadows flitting down that phantom polo ground;
You can hear the loud collisions as the flying players meet,
And the rattle of the mallets, and the rush of ponies' feet,
Till the terrified spectator rides like blazes to the pub —
He's been haunted by the spectres of the Geebung Polo Club.

THE NEVER-NEVER LAND

Henry Lawson

By homestead, hut, and shearing-shed,
  By railroad, coach, and track —
By lonely graves where rest our dead,
  Up Country and Out Back;
To where beneath the clustered stars
  The dreamy plains expand —
My home lies wide a thousand miles
  In the Never-Never Land.

[It lies beyond . . .

It lies beyond the farming-belts,
  Wide wastes of scrub and plain,
A blazing desert in the drought,
  A lake-land after rain;
To the skyline sweeps the waving grass,
  Or whirls the scorching sand —
A phantom land, a mystic realm!
  The Never-Never Land.

Where lone Mount Desolation lies,
  Mounts Dreadful and Despair,
'Tis lost beneath the rainless skies
  In hopeless deserts there;
It spreads nor'-west by No-Man's Land —
  Where clouds are seldom seen —
To where the cattle stations lie
  Three hundred miles between.

The drovers of the Great Stock Routes
  The strange Gulf Country know,
Where, travelling for the northern grass,
  The big lean bullocks go;
And camped by night where plains lie wide
  Like some old ocean's bed,
The stockmen in the starlight ride
  Round fifteen hundred head.

And west of named and numbered days
  The shearers walk and ride,
Jack Cornstalk and the Ne'er-do-well
  And Greybeard side by side;
They veil their eyes from moon and stars,
  And slumber on the sand —
Sad memories sleep as years go round
  In Never-Never Land.

O rebels to society!
  The Outcasts of the West —
O hopeless eyes that smile for me,
  And broken hearts that jest!
The pluck to face a thousand miles,
  The grit to see it through!
The communism perfected
  Till man to man is True.

The Arab to the desert sand,
  The Finn to fens and snow,
The "Flax-stick" dreams of Maoriland,
  While seasons come and go.
Whatever stars may glow or burn
  O'er lands of East and West,
The wandering heart of man will turn
  To one it loves the best.

Lest in the city I forget
  True mateship, after all,
My waterbag and billy yet
  Are hanging on the wall.
And I, to save my soul, again
  Would tramp to sunsets grand
With sad-eyed mates across the plain
  In the Never-Never Land.

ACKNOWLEDGEMENTS

The publishers have made every effort to seek permission for material in copyright but in some cases they have been unable to trace copyright owners. Should any infringement have occurred the publishers offer their apologies.

Grateful acknowledgement for permission to use copyright material is made to the following:
Angus & Robertson Publishers for C.J. Dennis's "The Intro" from *The Sentimental Bloke*, and "The Traveller" from *The Selected Verse of C.J. Dennis*; Rosemary Dobson's "Country Press" from *Rosemary Dobson: Selected Poems*, 1980; Mary Gilmore's "I Saw the Beauty Go" from *The Passionate Heart and Other Poems* and "Old Botany Bay" from *The Singing Tree*; P.J. Hartigan's "Around the Boree Log" and "Said Hanrahan" from *Around the Boree Log*; A.D. Hope's "Australia" from *Collected Poems 1930-1970*; Eve Langley's "Native Born" from *Modern Australian Verse*, ed. Douglas Stewart; Jack Moses's "Nine Miles from Gundagai" from *Nine Miles from Gundagai*; John Shaw Neilson's "The Sundowner" from *The Poems of Shaw Neilson*, ed. A.R. Chisholm; Will Ogilvie's "Drought", and "The Death of Ben Hall" from *From the Ballads to Brennan*, ed. T. Inglis Moore; Kenneth Slessor's "Country Towns" from *Selected Poems*; Douglas Stewart's "Place Names" from *Collected Poems, 1936-1967*; and Judith Wright's "South of My Days" and "Bullocky" from *Collected Poems 1942-1970*; Angus & Robertson Publishers and the copyright proprietor for A.B. Paterson's "Clancy of the Overflow", "Mulga Bill's Bicycle", "The Geebung Polo Club", "The Man From Snowy River" and "Waltzing Matilda" from *The Collected Verse of A.B. Paterson*; Nancy Cato for "Independence", Curtis Brown and the Estate of the late Dorothea Mackellar for Dorothea Mackellar's "High Places", "In a Southern Garden", "My Country" and "Spring on the Plains"; Roland Robinson for "White Birds" and "The Drovers".

Acknowledgement is gratefully made to the National Library of Australia for the use of photographs and illustrations from their collection.

Endpapers Rural view, Caire collection
Title page Sunday in the bush, *Town and Country Journal*, 1874
Page 1 Marysville, Caire collection
Page 8 Strayed from the picnic (detail), *Australian Sketcher*, 1875
Page 12 On the wallaby track
Page 16 Russells Hotel, Caire collection
Page 21 Andamooka Station
Page 32 Rounding up wild horses, *Australian*, 1870
Page 44 Bullock teams, Michael Kerry collection
Page 48 Hall of Commerce, Cootamundra Historical Society
Page 50 Allendale Station
Page 56 Interior of shearing shed, Riverina District
Page 66 Overlander rounding up a straggler, *Illustrated Australian News*, 1872
Page 70 Shearers at Currawillinghi
Page 80 Selectors' shearing shed on Birrie Creek near Brewarrina, 1890
Page 106 Shepherding in Australia, *Illustrated Australian News*, 1864
Page 110 Bullock driver, Kyogle, Michael Kerry collection
Page 114 Caire collection
Page 116 Todmorden Station, 1921, Senator Sir John Newlands' album
Page 120 On the wallaby track, album Winchombe Carson & Co.